Jordan

Case Study of a Pivotal State

Asher Susser

Policy Papers no. 53

THE WASHINGTON INSTITUTE FOR NEAR EAST POLICY

© 2000 by the Washington Institute for Near East Policy

Published in 2000 in the United States of America by the Washington Institute for Near East Policy, 1828 L Street NW, Suite 1050, Washington, DC 20036.

Library of Congress Cataloging-in-Publication Data

Susser, Asher.
    Jordan : a case study of a pivotal state / Asher Susser.
            p.   cm. — (Policy papers ; no. 53)
    Includes bibliographical references.
    ISBN 0-944029-37-X (pbk.)
    1. Jordan—Politics and government—1952-1999.
2. Jordan—Foreign relations—1952-1999. 3. Jordan—
Foreign relations—Israel. 4. Israel—Foreign relations—
Jordan. 5. Arab-Israeli conflict—Jordan. I. Title.
II. Policy papers (Washington Institute for Near East
Policy) ; no. 53.
DS154.55 S88 2000
956.9504—dc21   00-023015
                                                     CIP
Cover photos of King 'Abdullah I and King 'Abdullah II
© Corbis. Cover photo of King Hussein courtesy of Majlis
el-Hassan. Cover design by Monica Neal Hertzman.

The Author

A sher Susser is a senior research fellow at the Moshe Dayan Center for Middle Eastern and African Studies, a former head of the center, and associate professor in the Department of Middle Eastern and African History at Tel Aviv University. His fields of specialization include the history and politics of Jordan and the Palestinians, and religion and state in the Middle East. Professor Susser's other Jordan-related works include *On Both Banks of the Jordan: A Political Biography of Wasfi al-Tall* (1994) and *The Hashemites in the Modern Arab World* (1995). He is also most recently the editor of *Six Days, Thirty Years: New Perspectives on the Six-Day War* (1999, in Hebrew).

Professor Susser was a 1996–97 visiting research fellow at The Washington Institute for Near East Policy.

• • •

Table of Contents

Acknowledgments

The research and writing for this project was set in motion during my three-month stay as a visiting fellow at The Washington Institute for Near East Policy from December 1996 to February 1997 and continued over parts of three subsequent summers in Israel. I am therefore deeply indebted to many people in different places for their assistance and goodwill, without which this work would never have been completed.

First and foremost I am especially grateful to the executive director of The Washington Institute, Dr. Robert Satloff, for the invitation to spend time at the Institute and for the friendship, cooperation, and research environment that he and his colleagues so graciously provided. It was a real pleasure, socially and intellectually, to have had such an opportunity. Things would not have fallen into place as they did without the helping hand of the ever-efficient Institute administrator, Nina Bisgyer, and my work would not have been possible without the regular input of Greg Saiontz, my tireless, patient, and always polite research assistant. I owe a special word of thanks to the director of publications, Monica Neal Hertzman, and her publications associate, Alicia Gansz, for editing the final manuscript. I am also most thankful to Adiba Mango, a Soref research fellow at the Institute, who read the manuscript and made some extremely valuable suggestions.

In Israel, my professional home has been at the Moshe Dayan Center, at Tel Aviv University, for over twenty-five years. Dr. Martin Kramer, the center's director, who has always been a good friend and support, and Amira Margalith, assistant to the director—another good friend and an institution in her own right—both deserve a hearty vote of gratitude, along with the rest of my colleagues, for the drive, initiative, collegial spirit, and scholarly atmosphere that make the center the research haven that it is. Research at the Dayan Center, generally speaking and for this project in particular, owes very much to Haim Gal and Marion Gliksberg, those good people who run our press archives, documentation center, and library. My thanks are also due to another Dayan Center institution, Lydia Gareh, who toiled so diligently in transferring the text from one program to another, until all was finally set.

I would also like to thank the librarians at the Israel State Archives and the U.S. Cultural Center in Jerusalem for their assistance, and especially my good friend, Dr. Zaki Shalom, from Ben Gurion University, who graciously permitted me to quote from an unpublished manuscript of his own work.

Finally, although indebted to many, any mistakes or flaws that may remain in this work are solely my own.

Asher Susser
Tel Aviv
May 2000

Preface

W "here you stand," says the adage, "depends on where you sit." That axiom has defined Jordanian national security strategy from its inception as the Emirate of Trans-Jordan eighty years ago to its present-day form as the Hashemite Kingdom. And given Jordan's key role in all major Middle East policy questions—from the peace process to Iraq to the fight against Islamic extremism—assessing Jordan's "geostrategic centrality" is essential to sound planning on each of these critical issues. Indeed, understanding the fundamentals of Jordanian security strategy is especially important given the death of its legendary monarch, King Hussein, and the accession of his eldest son, King 'Abdallah II.

To review the evolution of Jordan's regional role and identify areas of continuity and change over the years, The Washington Institute is proud once again to present the work of Professor Asher Susser. Professor Susser, senior research fellow and former director of the Moshe Dayan Center for Middle Eastern and African Studies at Tel Aviv University, is widely recognized as one of the world's leading experts on Jordanian history, politics, and society. This is the third Washington Institute Policy Paper on Jordan he has written over the past fifteen years, a testament both to the enduring importance of Jordan to regional affairs and Professor Susser's authoritative voice on all things Jordanian.

As Jordan enters a new era—and as the Middle East itself teeters precariously between peace and conflict—we are pleased to present this timely and important work.

Michael Stein
Chairman

Fred S. Lafer
President

Author's Note

The term "pivotal state" has been borrowed from Joseph Nevo and Ilan Pappe, eds., *Jordan in the Middle East, 1948–1988: The Making of a Pivotal State* (London: Frank Cass, 1994).

Executive Summary

The stability of the Hashemite Kingdom has consistently confounded observers. Jordan has been perceived as particularly artificial and thus inherently less viable than other Fertile Crescent states. Its imminent demise has been predicted time and again only to be defied by its seemingly extraordinary capacity to endure and remain one of the most stable states in the Middle East. There are, of course, a variety of explanations for Jordan's longevity, not the least of which is the political astuteness, acumen, and courage of its monarchs.

The death of King Hussein, therefore, gave rise to renewed doubt and speculation about Jordan's stability, yet these apprehensions were dispelled by the smooth transition from Hussein to 'Abdallah II. In the popular view, Jordan's very existence had come to be so intimately identified with Hussein's person that many questioned whether the monarchy could survive his passing. However widespread, this view tended to ignore the overriding historical factors, above and beyond the personality of the monarch, which have contributed to Jordan's longevity. 'Abdallah I and Hussein provided leadership, maintained elite cohesion, and served as the "unifying essence" of the political order—and, as such, they were of immeasurable importance at critical junctures. But Jordan has never been a one-man show, and above and beyond the role and personality of its monarchs, a variety of other factors have contributed to the unexpected longevity of the Hashemite Kingdom. One such factor is the kingdom's geopolitical centrality. As a pivotal state to the stability of the region, Jordan has consistently stimulated the interest of external powers, both in the region and beyond, in the kingdom's continued well-being as an essential component of the regional status quo.

This last element has been a major determinant in the kingdom's own foreign policy and in the policies of other regional and nonregional actors toward Jordan, both before and after Hussein, and is the focus of this study. As Jordan is situated at the "strategic core" of the Fertile Crescent—between Israel and Iraq, Syria and Saudi Arabia, and at the heart of the Palestinian question—its destabilization could have potentially horrendous consequences for the region as a whole. But more often than not, Jordan's geopolitical centrality has proven an asset rather than a liability to its own interests and is thus a central facet of, and explanation for, the kingdom's remarkable longevity.

References by Jordanian leaders to the kingdom being located in a "killing zone," or to its "geopolitically thankless position," reflect Jordan's encirclement by neighbors that are relatively more powerful and capable of inflicting a wide array of extremely damaging penalties on the vulnerable kingdom—from political subversion, economic sanctions, or blockades, to "demographic aggression" or outright military invasion and conquest. Jordan, therefore, depends on the development of strong political and economic ties with an external power, and always with at least some of its neighbors, to ensure its survival.

Yet this very same geopolitical centrality, as an asset rather than a liability, has afforded Jordan the essential room to maneuver to secure its interests. Its long border with Israel lends the kingdom crucial importance to its Arab neighbors during both peace and war. Jordan's Arab neighbors tend to see the kingdom as a potential bridge to Israeli penetration of the Arab world or as an Arab asset in promoting Israeli isolation. In both cases, Jordan may potentially benefit rather than suffer from the attentions of its neighbors. Jordanian leaders, analysts, and commentators refer time and again to the advantages inherent in the kingdom's pivotal location, lending it an importance in terms of regional security or trade that is greater than its size, intrinsic power, or wealth would normally warrant.

During the last fifty years, the frequently underestimated resilience of the Hashemites, together with the strategic backing and subvention of those supporting the status quo in Jordan, have outweighed the political hostility, military threats, economic sanctions, and subversion of the kingdom's opponents. All these factors explain not only the prolonged stability of the state but also the regime's enhanced image as a survivor. This image, in turn, has augmented the regime's deterrence against its domestic opponents, who have at times been restrained by the possibility—real or imagined—of foreign intervention when the regime seemed seriously endangered.

Jordan's geopolitical centrality has indeed accorded the kingdom a strategic importance that has remained intact in the face of frequently changing circumstances. Trans-Jordan initially had little meaning beyond its importance to British strategy and imperial communications, and its significance naturally declined when British interests changed or when British power itself receded. But the Arab–Israeli conflict and the struggle for Palestine reaffirmed the kingdom's pivotal role for additional reasons. For instance, Jordan's utility to Israel as a *cordon sanitaire* was almost equaled by the importance that Israel's adversaries in the Arab world attached to the kingdom as a platform for the invasion of Israel or, alternatively, as an indirect approach for an Israeli attack on Syria. Although Jordan's military is not the most powerful in the region by a wide margin, it is certainly the most highly respected and professional military force in the Arab world. The strategic importance of Jordanian territory, together with its military power, have therefore been almost as crucial to Syria as they have been to Israel, albeit for diametrically opposing reasons.

The almost universal recognition of Jordan's geopolitical centrality and its concomitant stabilizing effect on the mosaic of Middle Eastern states has evolved over time. Whether it will continue to exist in the long run is a moot question. Nevertheless, one might risk an assessment. Considering the historical record, the inherent vagaries and volatility of regional politics, and the dependence of external states on the area's resources, it is quite likely that Jordanian stability will continue to be of paramount interest to major powers both inside and outside the region. For most states, the Hashemite regime is preferable to any of the alternatives—fundamentalist or otherwise. Moreover, a collapse of the regime and the violent scramble for the spoils that would likely ensue between Syria and Iraq, or between either one—or both together—against Israel, is hardly a welcome prospect. Few, if any, have an interest in such a catastrophic turn of events.

Jordan is no longer needed as a barrier against Arab revolutionaries or Soviet expansionism. But the kingdom's role as regional stabilizer among the Fertile Crescent states and between Arabs and Israelis remains as crucial as ever. Indeed, the impressive turnout of foreign dignitaries for King Hussein's funeral in February 1999, one of the largest gatherings of world leaders ever seen, was more than a gesture of respect to a great leader. It was an unprecedented demonstration of support by the international community for Jordan's well-being. In light of the historical record, the smooth transition from Hussein to 'Abdallah II should come as no surprise. External interest in Jordan's continued stability, the cohesion of the country's ruling elite, and the loyalty of the security establishment and armed forces to the existing political order have been prime factors ensuring more than just success in the transition of power. They explain the overall historical longevity and stability of the Hashemite Kingdom of Jordan.

Introduction

The stability of the Hashemite Kingdom has consistently confounded observers. Characterized by one historian as "a political anomaly and a geographical nonsense,"1 Jordan has been perceived as particularly artificial and thus inherently less viable than other Fertile Crescent states. Its imminent demise has been predicted time and again, only to be defied by the seemingly extraordinary capacity to endure and remain one of the most stable states in the region. There are, of course, a variety of explanations for Jordan's longevity, not the least of which is the political astuteness, acumen, and courage of its monarchs.

Indeed, the Jordanian monarchy has proven one of the most resilient regimes in the modern Middle East. The kingdom has been blessed with two particularly astute kings—'Abdallah I, founder of the kingdom, and Hussein, creator of modern Jordan—who were talented, courageous, and pragmatic practitioners of the craft of politics and the art of diplomacy. King Hussein, for example, ruled Jordan for forty-six years, from his assumption of power in May 1953 until his death at the age of 63 in February 1999. In July 1958, shortly after the overthrow of the Hashemite monarchy in Iraq, Anthony Nutting, Britain's former minister of state for foreign affairs, observed, "However much one may admire the courage of this lonely young king [Hussein], it is difficult to avoid the conclusion [that] his days are numbered."2 But more than forty years elapsed, and Hussein finally succumbed to cancer—not to his political rivals.

If the death of King Hussein gave rise to renewed doubt and speculation about Jordan's stability, these hesitations were dispelled by the smooth transition from Hussein to 'Abdallah II. In the popular view, Jordan's very existence had come to

1

be so intimately identified with Hussein's person that many questioned whether the monarchy could survive his passing. Yet however widespread, this view tended to ignore the over-riding historical factors, above and beyond the personality of the monarch, that have contributed to Jordan's longevity. 'Abdallah I and Hussein provided leadership, maintained elite cohesion, and served as the "unifying essence" of the political order—and, as such, they were of immeasurable importance at critical junctures. But Jordan has never been a one-man show, and above and beyond the role and personality of its monarchs, a variety of other factors have contributed to the unexpected longevity of the Hashemite Kingdom:

- the evolution and crystallization of a cohesive civilian and military elite known as the "King's men," supported by a stable and sufficiently broad power base and motivated by self-interest in preserving the status quo as well as their political patrimony;
- the loyalty of the armed forces and the domestic security establishment, which is largely a function of cohesion among the civilian and military elite;
- the comparative weakness of the regime's opponents from within and the irresolution of those from without;
- the relative homogeneity of the population, the vast majority of whom are Sunni Muslim Arabs (the cleavage between Palestinians and Jordanians—neither religious nor ethnic—is a relatively novel and historically shallow phenomenon, in no way comparable to the cleavages between Muslims and Christians, Sunnis and Shi'is, or Arabs and Kurds that plague other Arab states and have existed for centuries); and
- the kingdom's geopolitical centrality as a state pivotal to regional stability, which has consistently stimulated the interest of external powers—both in the region and beyond—in Jordan's continued well-being.[3]

This last element has been a major determinant in the kingdom's own foreign policy and in the policies of other regional and nonregional actors toward Jordan, both before and after Hussein, and will serve as the focus of this study. As Jordan is situated at the "strategic core" of the Fertile Crescent—between Israel and Iraq, Syria and Saudi Arabia, and at the heart of the Palestinian question—its destabilization could have potentially horrendous consequences for the region as a whole. But more often than not, Jordan's geopolitical centrality has proven an asset to its own interests rather than a liability, and is thus a central facet of, and explanation for, the kingdom's remarkable longevity.

Notes

1. Avi Shlaim, *Collusion Across the Jordan: King 'Abdullah, the Zionist Movement, and the Partition of Palestine* (Oxford: Clarendon Press, 1988), p. 31.

2. Uriel Dann, *King Hussein and the Challenge of Arab Radicalism: Jordan, 1955–1967* (New York, Oxford: Oxford University Press, 1989), epigraph.

3. Dann, pp. 165–169; Robert Satloff, *From 'Abdullah to Hussein: Jordan in Transition* (New York: Oxford University Press, 1994), pp. 174–175; Asher Susser, *On Both Banks of the Jordan: A Political Biography of Wasfi al-Tall* (London: Frank Cass, 1994), pp. 176–181.

Chapter 1

An Artificial Creation

The Kingdom of Jordan is, in fact, an artificial creation, in some respects more so than are its neighbors. With a tiny, primarily rural and tribal population, no urban center to speak of, and scarcely any resources—natural or otherwise— this dusty backwater did not appear to have much of a future when it achieved statehood in the spring of 1921. Even Emir 'Abdallah, the country's own founder, and later king, was never truly happy with his lot. He envied his younger brother, Faisal, who became king of Iraq—the country of the great Tigris and Euphrates rivers, and with Baghdad, the historical capital of the Abbasids, at its center. Amman, by contrast, was no more than a little Circassian village of some two thousand inhabitants at the time, and 'Abdallah, having been saddled with a territory no one wanted, declared not long after his arrival that he had "had enough of this wilderness of Trans-Jordania."[1] Indeed, Trans-Jordan had little value in its own right for 'Abdallah; it was but a stepping stone to greater things. His sights were set on expansion, preferably to include all of Greater Syria and the Hijaz, and at least Palestine. For 'Abdallah, the center of the Arab world was Greater Syria with Damascus at its core, which he saw as one naturally unified country whose partition, to him, was fundamentally illegitimate.

Needless to say, the separate existence of Trans-Jordan was hardly self-evident to the emir. And if this were true for 'Abdallah, its founding leader, it was certainly true for others. After 'Abdallah's assassination in 1951, there was no obviously capable successor in sight: his elder son, Talal, was mentally ill; his other son, Nayif, was incompetent; and his grandson, Hussein, was but a youngster of sixteen. Profound uncertainty prevailed in many quarters over the persistence of Jordan as an independent entity, and the dissolution of the kingdom was a widely discussed item on the regional agenda. Iraq, then still a Hashemite monarchy, "engaged in intensive efforts to bring Jordan under its patronage" by proposing a union between the two states.[2] Meanwhile the Saudis—who in the not-too-distant past had advanced claims to Ma'an and Aqaba in southern Jordan and were always on the lookout to block Hashemite attempts at aggrandizement—suggested a partition of their own between themselves and the Syrians, who would take the northern part of Jordan while the Saudis would keep the southern part.[3]

Five years later, during the turbulent early years of Hussein's reign and at the height of the 1956 Suez Crisis, the Iraqi, Syrian, and Saudi regimes stationed troops in Jordan as a precautionary measure. When the crisis subsided, the Iraqis immediately withdrew, but the Syrians and the Saudis took their time. According to the British ambassador at the time, Charles Johnston, their delay "gave the unsettling impression that they were simply pre-positioned there to ensure the best results for their countries in an eventual carve-up of Jordanian territory."[4]

In his own heyday, Egyptian president Gamal Abdul Nasser had nothing but derision and contempt for Jordan and its king. Moreover, the incipient Palestine Liberation Organization (PLO), still very much under Nasser's aegis, repeatedly challenged the kingdom's right to exist, considering it as nothing more than a colonialist fabrication. Ahmad al-Shuqayri, the PLO's first chairman, dismissed Jordan as a country that lacked "the principal foundations of statehood" and said that its separation from Palestine had no historical justification, as Palestine's true boundaries stretched from "the Mediterranean Sea in the west" to the "Iraqi and Syrian deserts" in the east.[5] Even after it gained independence from Nasser, the PLO, at least initially, did not much alter its perception of Jordan as an integral part of historical Palestine, detached by colonial fiat to serve the interests of Zionism.[6]

Somewhat more surprising was the case made against Jordan, as late as 1973, by the moderate, pro-Western president of Tunisia, Habib Bourguiba. Urging the Palestinians to adopt a more realistic set of demands in their conflict with Israel, Bourguiba suggested that they accept the partition resolution of 1947 as the basis for their independent state. When asked whether he thought Jordan would find such a partition acceptable—considering that the kingdom still claimed the West Bank as its own—Bourguiba replied that it did not really matter what the Jordanians were willing to accept. Jordan, he said, was "just another part of Palestine called Trans-Jordan" and was, after all, an "artificial issue" *(qadiyya mustana'a)*.[7]

With the stabilization of the Arab state system in the late 1960s and early 1970s onward, however, the attacks on Jordan's legitimacy gradually receded—only to be picked up by right-wing elements in Israel, who, for reasons of their own, began to argue that "Jordan is Palestine." Although it had lost much of its potency and relevance in an Arab world no longer governed by militant pan-Arabism, the campaign to delegitimize Jordan was still alive and well.

The conventional wisdom that Jordan was more artificial than other states in the region carried with it the assumption that, sooner or later, the kingdom would be swept away by the forces of history. This assumption, however, as one former British ambassador put it, not only "underestimated the resilience of the Jordanian monarchy" but even more importantly tended to ignore the reasoning behind the establishment of the state.[8] True, at its inception, Jordan was the relatively insignificant extension of Syria to the north, Palestine (later Israel) to the west, and the Arabian Peninsula (later Saudi Arabia) to the south. But it was precisely this location that would later accord the kingdom its true importance, far beyond anything its meager resources and small population might have suggested. At the core of the Fertile Crescent and physically closest of all Arab states to the epicenter of the emerging conflict in Palestine, Trans-Jordan (and later Jordan) was to assume the role of regional stabilizer, or shock absorber, that other actors near and far could not afford to dismiss.

Indeed, its strategic location gave the kingdom its "greatest value in the eyes of outside powers . . . [and] an importance of which most small and natural resource under-endowed states could only dream." Consequently, although dependent on external revenue since its inception, Jordan has generally "managed over the years to extract financial support of various kinds from concerned states" in the Middle East and outside the region.[9] The small size of the Jordanian economy has furthermore made it possible for these states to provide the necessary support at relatively low cost.

At first, however, as Mary Wilson suggests, "Trans-Jordan's existence hinged on European interests rather than on a local or regional rationale."[10] The British originally believed that once things in Palestine "settled down," Trans-Jordan could more easily be administered as an Arab district of Palestine. But matters in Palestine did not settle down, and as the Jewish–Arab conflict intensified in the 1930s, the advantages of Trans-Jordanian separateness became increasingly apparent.

In fact, British strategists began to think of Trans-Jordan as a useful entity in and of itself. For example, the kingdom concurrently isolated a conflict-ridden Palestine from other areas of British interest, and served as a barrier against Saudi–Wahhabi militancy toward both Palestine and Syria, which was then under the control of Britain's French allies. It also provided a secure air and land corridor between Britain's possessions in the eastern Mediterranean and the Gulf, and was thus recognized as "a geographical barrier whose distinct political circumstances served Britain's interests." Although it viewed Jordan "more as a buffer to Palestine than as a country capable of development in itself," Britain regarded the money used for the kingdom's upkeep and stability as well spent, considering the much more expensive alternatives.[11] In later years, although circumstances changed time and again, Jordan's role as a regional stabilizer would continue to be recognized by Britain, as well as by the United States, Germany, a variety of Arab states, Israel, Japan, and others.

Geopolitical Centrality: Liability and Asset

When Iraq made its previously mentioned advances toward Jordan in 1951, it was rebuffed by the Jordanian political elite, jealous of their own prerogatives and confident of their country's viability and independence. Iraq was similarly deterred by a formidable array of Arab and other states, all opposed to any change in the regional balance of power. The Saudis were especially active in mobilizing opposition to Iraq's absorption of Jordan, instead disseminating propaganda in favor of Syria's own ambitions for the kingdom, even if only as a tactical anti-Iraqi ploy. Moreover, the Saudis approached both the British and the Americans, seeking assurances of support for the regional status quo. With the giving of these assurances, "ironically, the continued independent existence and well-being of the most 'artificial' of all the Arab entities established after World War I . . . was now deemed vital by the non-Hashemite Arab states."[12]

Jordan's geopolitical centrality has indeed exposed the kingdom to a wide variety of pressures from its more powerful neighbors: frontal military attack, economic sanctions and blockades, subversion and terrorism, manipulation of its domestic politics, and the demographic pressures of refugees, both from the conflict with neighboring Israel and more recently from Iraq. Moreover, as a relatively weak state, Jordan does not have the power to shape the regional context in which it functions. It is consequently influenced by regional trends—ideological, political, or economic—over which it has little or no control. Former Crown Prince Hassan likened the challenges inherent in Jordan's location to "living in the eye of an ever-blowing storm."[13]

This very same situation, however, is also one of political, strategic, and economic opportunity. Tawfiq Abu al-Huda, one of Jordan's most strong-minded and capable prime ministers, served in the time of 'Abdallah I and also during Hussein's early years and was the first Jordanian statesman to appreciate the value inherent in Jordan's structural weaknesses. The kingdom's "need for outside protection, its swollen refugee population, its inadequate economic base, its long frontier with Israel, and, of course, its control of only part of the land west of the Jordan River, could be turned into valuable political (and economic) assets. The monies that foreign donors . . . and, eventually, other Arab states paid to Jordan were, after all, a function of Jordan's frailty, not its strength."[14] In later years, it was again Prince Hassan who observed that Jordan stood to gain if it could only reap the fruits of its status as "*terra media* between Israel on the Mediterranean coast and the oil-rich states" of the Arabian Peninsula and the Gulf. As suggested by one of Hassan's advisors, Jordan had the capacity to become "the pivot of peace" instead of "a buffer between enemies," its more traditional function.[15]

Since the mid-1950s, Jordan has faced a series of conflicting pressures on countless issues, as competing powers have struggled for regional control or domination. Jordan's position between Israel and Iraq, its long border with Israel, and its large Palestinian population have made the kingdom a primary target both for the revolutionaries who sought to overturn the status quo there, and for the conservatives who wished to preserve it. Britain, Hashemite Iraq, and Turkey, for example, made an effort to draw Jordan into the anti-Soviet Baghdad Pact in 1955, only to be thwarted by popular pro-Nasserist sentiment, Egyptian subversion, and Nasser's skillful manipulation of Jordan's volatile domestic scene.[16] Hussein tried briefly to ride the Nasserist wave and nearly lost his throne in the process. In early 1957, the king finally faced down domestic opposition, buttressed by the generous support of the United States, who had stepped into the shoes of the departing British as the leading Western power in the region and Jordan's main source of financial support. The new American role was adopted despite Secretary of State John Foster Dulles's conclusion only months before that "Jordan had no justification as a state."[17] The United States was now acting with regard to the kingdom the way it had elsewhere in the region, such as in Greece or Turkey, "stepp[ing] in financially to prevent collapse and perhaps chaos in Jordan which could have brought on an area-wide crisis, the consequences of which could well have been disastrous not only for Jordan but for the region as a whole."[18]

Notes

1. Kamal Salibi, *The Modern History of Jordan* (London: I. B. Tauris, 1993), p. 95.

2. Bruce Maddy-Weitzman, "Jordan and Iraq: Efforts at Intra-Hashemite Unity," *Middle Eastern Studies* 26, no. 1 (1990), p. 66.

3. Bruce Maddy-Weitzman, *The Crystallization of the Arab State System, 1945–1954* (Syracuse: Syracuse University Press, 1993), p. 32; Avi Shlaim, *Collusion Across the Jordan: King 'Abdullah, the Zionist Movement, and the Partition of Palestine* (Oxford: Clarendon Press, 1988), p. 608.

4. Charles Johnston, *The Brink of Jordan* (London: Hamish Hamilton, 1972), p. 23.

5. Asher Susser, *On Both Banks of the Jordan: A Political Biography of Wasfi al-Tall* (London: Frank Cass, 1994), pp. 101–102.

6. Yehoshafat Harkabi, ed., *The Arabs and Israel*, vols. 3–4, *The Resolutions of the Palestinian National Council* (in Hebrew) (Jerusalem: The Truman Institute, Hebrew University, 1975), pp. 166, 184.

7. Interview with Habib Bourguiba in *al-Nahar*, July 6, 1973.

8. Johnston, *The Brink of Jordan*, p. 117.

9. Laurie Brand, *Jordan's Inter-Arab Relations: The Political Economy of Alliance Making* (New York: Columbia University Press, 1994), pp. 41–42.

10. Mary Wilson, *King 'Abdullah, Britain and the Making of Jordan* (New York: Cambridge University Press, 1987), p. 58.

11. Wilson, *King Abdullah*, pp. 70–71; Schirin Fathi, *Jordan–An Invented Nation? Tribe-State Dynamics and the Formation of National Identity* (Hamburg: Deutsches Orient–Institut, 1994), p. 89.

12. Maddy-Weitzman, "Jordan and Iraq," pp. 68–69; Robert Satloff, *From 'Abdullah to Hussein: Jordan in Transition* (New York: Oxford University Press, 1994), pp. 33–34.

13. Satloff, *From 'Abdullah to Hussein*, p. 45.

14. Ibid.

15. Hassan Bin Talal, "Return to Geneva," *Foreign Policy*, no. 57 (Winter

1984–85), pp. 8, 12; Cecil Hourani, "Jordan's Role in the New Middle East: Central or Marginal?" *Jordan Times*, October 29, 1995.

16. Satloff, *From 'Abdullah to Hussein*, pp. 108–125.

17. Ibid., p. 158.

18. Report from U.S. Embassy Amman to Department of State Washington, September 5, 1959, in *Foreign Relations of the United States (FRUS) 1958–1960*, vol. 11, *Lebanon and Jordan*, p. 719.

Chapter 2
The Evolving Posture of Israel
and the Western Powers

It is commonly believed, and generally correct, that Israel
has consistently supported the status quo in Jordan. Israel's
first prime minister, David Ben-Gurion, firmly opposed Egyptian president Gamal Abdul Nasser's ambition of the early
1950s to create territorial contiguity between Egypt and Jordan through the Negev in southern Israel. Ben-Gurion was
similarly opposed to the possible stationing of Iraqi forces in
Jordan. Both of these positions were motivated by Israeli security concerns but had the simultaneous effect of shoring
up Jordanian sovereignty and independence in the face of
Egyptian or Iraqi expansionist designs. But at the same time,
Israel's leadership in the early 1950s, including Ben-Gurion
and Foreign Minister Moshe Sharett, remained extremely
skeptical about Jordan's viability, as did many others, both
then and thereafter. Ben-Gurion thought that "Trans-Jordan
was not something stable and natural, but [just] one man
['Abdallah], who could die at any moment, and [who] was
entirely dependent on England. . . ." Sharett, for his part,
believed Jordan might disappear and be swallowed up by Syria
or Iraq.[1] It should, therefore, come as no surprise that at a
number of critical junctures in Jordan's history, Ben-Gurion
seriously contemplated preemptive action to keep the West
Bank from falling into the hands of forces perceived to be
particularly hostile toward Israel.

The first of these junctures came after the assassination
of King 'Abdallah in July 1951, when Ben-Gurion briefly considered occupying all of the West Bank up to the Jordan River.
The second came in October 1956 during the Suez Crisis,

when the young King Hussein appeared to be falling into the hands of his pro-Nasserist domestic opposition. In a discussion with French premier Guy Mollet, Ben-Gurion proposed that Jordan be partitioned between Israel and Iraq. Israel would take possession of the West Bank, and Iraq the East Bank, provided Iraq sign a peace treaty with Israel and agree to absorb a large number of Palestinian refugees.[2]

A variation of this idea was proposed again in July 1958, just days after the Hashemite monarchy was overthrown in Iraq. Ben-Gurion dispatched two senior officials from the Israeli foreign ministry—Abba Eban and Reuven Shiloah—for secret talks in London with U.S. secretary of state John Foster Dulles. The Israelis were authorized to communicate the prime minister's opinion that there was "a better alternative to the continued separate existence of Jordan." If the status quo could no longer be maintained, they suggested, it might be possible to bring about a union between Iraq and the kingdom's East Bank, with some kind of autonomy in the West Bank, possibly united with Israel.[3]

The Change in Israeli Thinking on Jordan

It was precisely at this juncture, however, that Israeli thinking about Jordan began to assume a more coherent and consistent pattern. The measure of doubt concerning the kingdom's viability or the advantages of Jordan's separate existence yielded to the firm conviction that Jordan's independence was an Israeli interest. Even Ben-Gurion's directives to Eban and Shiloah were couched in cautious language, suggesting an alternative to the preservation of Hashemite sovereignty only if the status quo could not be maintained. Israel, as Ben-Gurion clarified to Eban, had no intention of exploiting the sorry state of affairs in Jordan.[4]

From an Israeli standpoint, regional developments had taken a serious turn for the worse. Nasser and his pro-Soviet, anti-Western, and virulently anti-Israeli brand of radical Arab nationalism were viewed in Israel with trepidation, especially as the Egyptian leader now appeared to be at the zenith of his power, on the verge of sweeping through the region in an unprecedented wave of success. Syria was firmly ensconced in Nasser's orbit, having joined with Egypt in the United Arab Republic (UAR) in February 1958; the anti-Nasserist Hashemite monarchy in Iraq had been overthrown; and pro-Western, Christian-dominated Lebanon was in turmoil as the pro-Nasserists there challenged the status quo in the first Lebanese civil war. The landings of U.S. Marines in Lebanon and British paratroopers in Jordan did help to stabilize the situation, but the Israelis were nevertheless desperate to find allies in the region to stem the Nasserist tide.

Quite naturally, Israel looked first to the non-Arab periphery of the Middle East—Turkey, Iran, and Ethiopia. Yet, among the countries of the Arab core, it was becoming increasingly apparent that only Jordan shared a vital interest with Israel in stopping Nasser. For the Hashemite Kingdom, the Egyptian leader was anathema, representing everything that Jordan did not. Anti-Western, anti-monarchical, revolutionary, and subversive, Nasser was an implacable foe whose influence the Jordanian regime genuinely feared. This was particularly true because of the Egyptian leader's messianic appeal to the kingdom's Palestinian majority and his alarming ability to mobilize them against their own government. As Uriel Dann has said, "It was [Nasser] whom Hussein came to regard as the incarnation of the forces embattled against himself."[5] This was a zero-sum game. Nasser's gains were Jordan's losses and vice versa; indeed, the same could have been said for Israel.

In the Israeli view, Jordan—having weathered yet another storm—seemed more resilient than hitherto perceived and therefore a more likely building block in any regional anti-Nasserist configuration. From the second half of 1958 onward, Israel's policy toward the kingdom began to develop into one of active and consistent support for Jordan's independence and territorial integrity. No longer regarding the country as a historical aberration that could disintegrate at any moment, Ben-Gurion had become convinced that an independent Jordan could serve as an effective bulwark against Nasserism. If, in the not-too-distant past, the United States had on occasion warned Israel against taking action detrimental to Jordan, the tables were now turned, and it was Israel that would begin urging U.S. protection of Jordan's sovereignty.[6]

Even before this noticeable change in Israeli posture, however, it had become clear to the Western powers that "Jordan's survival as an independent state was essential if peace was to be preserved" between the Arab states and Israel.[7] Considering Israel's sensitivity to the presence of foreign Arab forces on Jordanian territory, especially in the West Bank, the collapse of the kingdom might have led to a regional explosion. Especially with Israel's position evolving to one of more activist support for Jordanian integrity, it became clear to all that "a take-over in Jordan by Nasser would have entailed an Israeli reaction, which in turn could have precipitated an uncontrollable crisis."[8] According to Charles Johnston, this inspired Anglo–American aid to Jordan as a "cheap insurance policy against a definite risk of war," and it also deterred Nasser from taking rash action.[9]

In any case, Hussein and Jordan were never as important to Nasser as Egypt and Nasser were to Hussein. The difficulties inherent in the kingdom's economic and strategic situation "were well enough known to inspire hesitation in potential aggressors," as neither Egypt's Nasser nor Iraq's new president 'Abd al-Karim Qasim "wished to complicate their existing problems further by creating an immediate condition of chaos in Jordan."[10] Even so, "time and again, a purposeful lead by Abdel Nasser might have made the difference between Hussein's overthrow and a mere coup attempt, or a 'coup situation' that was not utilized."[11]

The Challenge of the UAR and Jordanian–Israeli Common Interest

What was invariably true of Nasser, however, was not always true of his subordinates. In August 1960, Jordan's outspoken anti-Nasserist prime minister, Hazza' al-Majali, was assassinated in an explosion that buried him and many others under the rubble of his office.[12] Col. 'Abd al-Hamid Sarraj, chairman of the executive council of the UAR's Northern Region (Syria) and chief of Syrian intelligence, was considered a prime suspect. But the extent of Egyptian involvement was not clear, and Hussein momentarily entertained the idea of military retaliation against Syria (not an unreasonable response at the time, given the military balance between the two countries). Israel's policy toward Jordan and the common cause the two countries shared in containing Nasser could hardly have gone unnoticed by the king. It was, therefore, not entirely surprising that Hussein made a discreet approach to the Israelis seeking a measure of coordination. In mid-September 1960, he sent a special emissary to meet with the chief of intelligence of the Israel Defense Forces (IDF) and inform him of Jordan's intentions with respect to Syria. The Israelis were specifically asked by the emissary not to exploit the deployment of Jordanian troops on the Syrian frontier by attacking the kingdom from the west.

In response, Prime Minister Ben-Gurion instructed that a message be relayed to the king in which Israel committed itself to take no action against Jordan. During the subsequent meeting between the chief of IDF intelligence and the king's emissary, the Israeli officer also assured his Jordanian interlocutor of what the Jordanians by now presumably already knew, "that the existence of an independent Jordan under the leadership of Hussein was an Israeli interest." To this, the Jordanian emissary replied that his country recognized the mutual interest Jordan and Israel had in each other's existence—a recognition that would serve as the foundation of an informal relationship existing for decades before a peace treaty would be concluded between the two states.[13]

Western Skepticism about Jordanian Longevity

In the late 1950s and early 1960s, this sense of common interest between Jordan and Israel was consolidated against a background of increasing skepticism about the kingdom's future in Britain and the United States—a skepticism that became even more pronounced after the formation of the UAR and the fall of the Hashemite regime in Iraq. A mood of reassessment fell over both London and Washington as the seemingly unstoppable current of Nasserism swept through the region. In both capitals, voices favoring accommodation with the regional forces most widely believed to be victorious in the future were increasing in number. Those forces were represented most authentically by Nasser. U.S. President John Kennedy and his advisers shared "the doctrinaire faith that postulated harmony between America's 'new frontiers' with the interests of a nationalistic Third World, and the view of the UAR accordingly as 'progressive.'"[14]

This trend was naturally corrosive to Jordan's stature in Western foreign policy bureaucracies, a revealing example of which is a statement of U.S. policy toward the Near East, drafted by the National Security Council (NSC) and approved by President Dwight Eisenhower in November 1958. Although still wary of expanding Nasserist influence in the region, these policy guidelines recommended normalizing relations with the UAR and exploring "the extent to which greater U.S. co-operation with the UAR might serve to limit UAR contacts with the Soviet Bloc." This, of course, would have immediate ramifications for U.S. policy toward Jordan. "Recognizing that the indefinite continuance of Jordan's present political status has been rendered unrealistic by recent developments," the guidelines stated, "and that attempts on [Washington's] part to support its continuance may also represent an obstacle to [the United States] establishing a working relationship with Arab nationalism," the United States should "seek . . . to bring about [the] peaceful evolution of Jordan's political status and to reduce the U.S. commitment in Jordan." The United States should, therefore, "encourage such peaceful political adjust-ment by Jordan, including partition, absorption, or internal political re-alignment, as appears desirable to the people of Jordan and as will permit improved relations with Jordan's Arab neighbors." It should similarly "seek to insure the peaceful acquiescence of Israel and of Jordan's Arab neighbors in any such adjustment"—that is, in Jordan's demise as an independent state, or at least in the removal of the Hashemite regime.[15]

This policy statement was by no means an isolated example of the pessimistic mood in Washington. According to the National Intelligence Estimate on Jordan for 1959, Jordan's existence "in the short run" was "bolstered by an uneasy equilibrium of external forces." In the long run, however, the assessment expressed "little confidence in Hussein's ability to hold his throne or, indeed, in the viability of Jordan as a state."[16] In the meantime, Israel continued to prefer Hussein to a pro-Nasserist alternative, and Nasser wanted to avoid a showdown with the West or war with Israel. But Hussein's best hope of retaining his throne for the longest period of time seemed to be in seeking peace with the pan-Arab nationalists—that is, with Nasser and his supporters in Jordan, even though an accord like this would probably not prove lasting. Said the estimate, "Eventually, it appears probable that [Hussein's] regime will give way, gradually or abruptly, to a successor more in tune with the political trends prevailing in the Arab world."[17]

In advance of Hussein's March 1959 visit to the United States, the State Department anticipated a concerted Jordanian effort "to extract from the U.S. assurances that [it was] firmly committed to the proposition that the continued existence of Jordan as it was then constituted was vital to the maintenance of the Western position in the Near East." While clarifying that it was not thinking of abandoning Jordan to "Nasser's tender mercies," the department nevertheless stated that it was simply "not possible for [Washington] to satisfy the desires and ambitions of the King." Instead, the United States "should seek to implant and cultivate in the King's mind the concept of a gradual and orderly rapprochement with the UAR. . . ."[18]

In June 1960, the policy guidelines of the NSC were updated by shedding some of the former convoluted language in favor of explicitly advocating "Jordan's peaceful evolution towards association with a larger Arab entity" and for the reduction of Washington's "financial burden in Jordan."[19] Reports from the Israeli embassy in Washington later that year (shortly after the assassination of Hazza' al-Majali) suggested a dejected consensus of opinion about Jordan among officials at the State Department. The situation in Jordan, they feared, was deteriorating; the king could be assassinated at any moment, and there was probably no alternative but to accept that the country was unsustainable and destined to disintegrate. At the same time, however, these officials recognized that Jordan could "not be sliced up peacefully," and that the United States, with little enthusiasm, would probably prop Jordan up if it had to.[20]

If Jordanians drew little hope from the Americans, neither did they draw much encouragement from their British friends. During a visit to London at the end of 1961, Hussein explained to his interlocutors that, as a leader completely identified with the West, he expected to receive public support from Britain both for himself and for his regime. He was politely rebuffed with the reply that Britain would continue to provide military and economic aid but publicly wished to maintain its position of neutrality between the Arab states. Hussein was even advised at this meeting to tone down Jordan's anti-Nasserist propaganda.[21] In a dispatch to London in early March 1962, the British ambassador in Amman expressed his doubts about the long-term survival of the Hashemite regime, recommending a policy of "disengagement, within very definite limits set by our interests." Like his colleagues in London, the ambassador went on to report that he had impressed upon the king the need to mend his fences with Nasser and even to "turn the other cheek when attacked."[22]

These developments obviously did not serve to bolster Hashemite confidence, nor did the widely held belief in Jordan, however incorrect, that the United States "was supporting Nasser's grand design." The regime was clearly disillusioned with the West and "intensely suspicious of American policy in the Middle East,"[23] as Hussein worried that an American appeasement of Nasser would strengthen Egypt's capacity to meddle in Jordan's domestic affairs.[24] The Israelis were similarly perturbed, and they made their position known to anyone prepared to listen, arguing that any policy of deference to Nasser was completely misguided. The natural course for the Western powers, they contended, was to support their true friends in the Arab world, chief of which was Jordan. In November 1960, for example, Foreign Minister Golda Meir told the French ambassador to Israel that she had difficulty understanding British and U.S. policy toward Jordan. The king was young, she granted, but he had already surprised the world with his courage and resilience. True, Jordan could not survive forever on handouts from the West, but neither should the kingdom be abandoned. Western powers should rather live up to their obligation to support Jordan and help it achieve economic independence.[25]

In their deliberations with the American administration during this period, the Israelis consistently made the case for continued aid to Jordan on the grounds that the kingdom—unlike the so-called revolutionary regimes—was engaged in relatively successful and peaceful economic and social reform. Furthermore and to its credit, the Israelis argued, Jordan kept the peace along the border with Israel, thus contributing to the regional stability in which the United States had such a fundamental interest.[26]

But the Western powers were still seeking some form of rapprochement with Nasser, and as a corollary were exhibiting less resolve and a disinclination to campaign openly on Jordan's behalf, much less to save the regime at all costs. Yet neither were they actively pursuing the kingdom's demise, for not everyone in Western foreign policy bureaucracies believed that such an outcome could avoid harming the interests of the West. For example, the U.S. embassy in Amman did not share "the pessimism about Jordan which, with reason, was fairly widespread in certain circles in Washington."[27] In September 1959, the embassy made a very strong case for "a continuation of the maintenance of Jordan as it is . . . with continued assistance from the U.S. and the UK." Without it, "there could easily be chaos, intervention [by Israel], and disaster." This kind of policy was to be considered "peace insurance," for which Washington had paid much higher premiums all over the world.[28] The line of argument must have had some effect. U.S. Assistant Secretary of State for Near Eastern and South Asian Affairs Phillips Talbot told the Senate Foreign Relations Committee in April 1962 that "the continued existence of Jordan as an independent political entity" was a "major factor in the maintenance of peace and stability in the area."[29] Although not a commitment to the Hashemite regime, this testimony was certainly at odds with the earlier policy direction of supporting Jordan's so-called "evolution toward association with a larger Arab entity."

The British ambassador's annual report on Jordan for 1962 included some indications of guarded optimism influenced by the sweeping domestic reforms introduced by Jordan's new, youthful, and energetic prime minister, Wasfi al-Tall. Although there was truth in the depiction of Jordan "as an anachronism," the ambassador observed, the kingdom was beginning to demonstrate "a capacity not only to survive against the odds but also to adapt itself in some measure to the wind of change."[30] British policy at the time was "not . . . to intervene" to save the regime, but to maintain "influence to prevent instability."[31] The British fully realized and accepted that they had "to pay for that [policy] in cash and in risking adverse publicity." Moreover, as was stated in a Foreign Office memorandum at the time, whereas "disengagement may be wise as a general direction it is doubtful whether it is to [Britain's] advantage to press on with it too fast."[32]

Jordanian Resolve and Israeli Determination

In the late 1950s and early 1960s, with Nasser still at the pinnacle of his power and regional influence, Western countries seemed to waver momentarily in their backing for Jordan. A number of factors combined to keep their support for the kingdom's integrity basically on course. First and foremost was the resolution and determination of the king and the local elite. Second, Nasser was not as determined to effect a Hashemite demise as the Jordanian regime was to protect itself. With the dissolution of the UAR in September 1961, Nasser's regional appeal began to decline as he met his first remarkable political and ideological defeat. Third, Nasser's setback had a restorative affect on the Western powers, which gradually let go their deterministic perceptions of Nasserist invincibility and inevitable triumph. (In the U.S. foreign policy establishment, the school that supported Jordan's absorption into a larger Arab entity was, no doubt, operating under the assumption that the UAR was the wave of the future—not the temporary aberration that it proved to be.)

Lastly, the role played by Israel in communicating the danger of any leaning by the West toward Nasser helped to secure continued support for the Hashemites from the Western powers. Even those who predicted Jordan's eventual demise believed it essential that this so-called "evolution of Jordan's political status" be secured with the peaceful acquiescence of Israel as well as Jordan's Arab neighbors. This was easier said than done, however, and Israel's protestations about the policies of the Western powers must have clearly suggested that Jordan's demise would have had anything but peaceful consequences. Israel thereby contributed to the eventual Western policy reformulation that Jordan's continued independence was a vital component of a stable regional order.

In stark contradiction to prevalent conspiracy theories, according to which the Great Powers have the mystical capacity to engineer regional politics, the story of the UAR, Jordan, and Israel proves quite the opposite. Whatever thoughts occupied the minds of analysts in Washington and London, the policies of the regional players and their relative successes or failures were, in the end, the decisive factors shaping Western thinking and policymaking toward the region. The mindset of the West was essentially preventive and defensive, concerned with safeguarding its own regional interests at minimum cost. Western powers therefore tended to bend with the winds emanating from the region far more than they actually determined the regional climate—the latter was Nasser's role, and the West responded according to the relative success either he or his adversaries were enjoying at any given moment. Key to the outcome of the contest with Nasser was therefore the resolve of Jordan, Israel, and Nasser's other regional foes to challenge him (each independently of the other).

Nasser's Last Hurrah: The Tripartite Union

The last round of this battle of wills was fought in April 1963, when a triumphant Nasser seemed for a fleeting moment to have once again captured the regional imagination. Jordan was thrust anew into a serious domestic crisis, and the questions surrounding its viability surfaced once more. In rapid succession, two Ba'thi coups were staged in early 1963, the first in Iraq (February 8) and the second in Syria (March 8). These coups set the stage for talks between the two new regimes and Nasser on the formation of a tripartite union of Syria, Iraq, and Egypt—talks which culminated in a declaration issued on April 17 proclaiming a new United Arab Republic. King Hussein was hence subjected yet again to the isolation and political suffocation he had been forced to endure in the days of the original UAR between Syria and Egypt. The self-assurance and concomitant aggressive posturing he had adopted toward Nasser since the breakup of the first UAR in September 1961 seemed to vanish without trace. Hussein appeared genuinely humbled by the Egyptian leader, now seemingly on the crest of a new wave of popularity and success, and the domestic opposition in Jordan was therefore duly emboldened.

By this time, the idea of Arab unity had an almost messianic appeal in the Arab world, especially for the Palestinians, who believed it to be both the precondition for and the precursor of "liberating the usurped homeland." The public in Jordan, as elsewhere in the Arab world, was gripped with euphoria. After the announcement of the tripartite union, mass rallies were staged throughout the West Bank and in the main cities of the East Bank demanding Jordan's immediate accession to the union. But the rallies soon turned into riots against the regime. Four demonstrators were killed by security forces in violence that broke out on April 20 in Jerusalem, a key flash point of the unrest. That same day, in the wake of the riots, the Jordanian prime minister lost the confidence of parliament and was forced to resign in the first and thus far last such instance in Jordan's history.[33] The regime appeared to be in serious trouble and the pessimistic assessments of U.S. analysts about the essential "evolution of Jordan's political status" seemed to be nearing realization.

Israel regarded the tripartite union as a potential threat to Jordan as well as to its own security, considering the combined power and avowedly hostile predisposition of all three union states. Following the West Bank demonstrations, Israel deployed reinforcements along its border with Jordan, and Prime Minister Ben-Gurion launched a diplomatic offensive with the Western powers to ensure their support for Jordan's independence, particularly after receiving alarming reports regarding American tendencies to acquiesce vis-à-vis Jordan's incorporation into the union.[34] Indeed, at the peak of the crisis there were, yet again, indications of American and British reluctance to oppose Nasser publicly, although these were hardly as blatant or telling as their indecisiveness two or three years earlier. Both powers were disinclined to take military action on Jordan's behalf against other Arab states (although, interestingly, they did consider intervening to counter an Israeli military action) but they were nevertheless determined to invest considerable diplomatic effort to ensure the kingdom's stability and integrity in the face of this latest pan-Arab challenge. [35]

Even so, the public posture of the Western powers during this period left much to be desired from the Jordanian point of view. At a foreign policy briefing on April 22, 1963, Assistant Secretary of State Talbot stated that U.S. support for

Jordan's continuity as a separate state lay both in its importance to regional stability and in its close ties with countries
outside the region, including the United States. Although a
positive, friendly gesture toward Jordan, this could hardly be
construed as a determined statement of public support; as
Uriel Dann noted, it simply did not require much effort "to
realize that 'a separate state' of Jordan [was] not synonymous
with 'the Hashemite Kingdom' and that Hussein, the linchpin of that kingdom and a known ally of the United States,
went unmentioned. The formulation of Talbot's announcement was undoubtedly carefully considered, in particular as
to what it left unsaid."[36]

Privately, however, both Britain and the United States
shared the view that Jordan's stability was essential, and that
the fall of a pro-Western regime like Hussein's ought to be
avoided. This, they assessed, was necessary to prevent instability from spreading from Jordan to the Arabian Peninsula,
thus endangering other pro-Western regimes—especially the
Saudi monarchy—to the detriment of Western standing in
the region and to the benefit of the Soviet Union. Stability in
Jordan was also necessary to avert the danger of another Arab–
Israeli war.[37]

A major reason for this assessment was the expectation in
both Britain and the United States that Israel would take preemptive military action in the event of a Nasserist-inspired
coup in Jordan—the underlying British assumption being that
ensuring the integrity of the Hashemite Kingdom and its regime was a vital Israeli interest of the first order. From the
Israeli viewpoint, the British Consul in Jerusalem observed,
Hashemite Jordan was a buffer against hostile Arab states,
and maintaining this buffer was one of Israel's fundamental
objectives. If Israel were to conclude that Jordan was about to
become a "cordon *in*sanitaire" it would take rapid action to
ensure a satisfactory alternative to the new situation.[38]

The Americans similarly believed that Israel would regard
the accession to power of a pro-Nasserist regime in Jordan
with "serious concern" and would probably prefer to make a

preemptive move "rather than risk the positioning of a non-Jordanian Arab force on her vulnerable eastern marches."[39] Were Israel not compelled to withdraw quickly, however, such an action could provoke an Arab response and set off a major crisis throughout the region.

Israel, for its part, appealed to President Kennedy to take necessary action to prevent the overthrow of King Hussein. Kennedy's response may not have been all Israel had hoped for, but he did recognize Israel's legitimate concerns. As a result, the United States further reassured Ben-Gurion that it would do its best to prevent the development of a dangerous situation in Jordan, while simultaneously cautioning Israel to show restraint and avoid precipitate action.[40] But Ben-Gurion had already decided against any major military operation; the Israeli deployment was more deliberately intended to deter Jordan's neighbors, an action which had its desired effect.

Still, according to American, British, and Israeli diplomatic correspondence at the time, the Egyptians were concerned that Israel would take military action in the event of a Hashemite fall. The United States, while continuing to warn the Israelis not to use force, therefore fully exploited the threat of Israeli military action in its communications with the Egyptians. In no uncertain terms, Washington warned the Egyptians that America would view with extreme disfavor any pro-Nasser subversion in Jordan, much less a pro-Nasser coup. Also impressed upon Egypt was the U.S. assessment that Israel would indeed occupy most or all of the West Bank in such an eventuality. Moreover, the Egyptians could not count on the United States to restrain Israel, and it would be "difficult to dislodge" the Israelis from the West Bank after such an action. Finally, the U.S. clarification to the Egyptians that they were "not relaying [an] Israeli threat, [but simply] recogniz[ing] reality," must have sounded particularly menacing. When the crisis subsided, both U.S. and British assessments concluded that the firm diplomatic stand taken by Washington, coupled with the threat of Israeli military intervention, had been a stabilizing factor deterring Nasser not only from military action but also from political subversion in Jordan. The threat of Israeli intervention also had a restraining effect on the Palestinians in Jordan, who feared that their own contribution to the destabilization of the regime might result in Israeli occupation.[41]

This crisis of April 1963 was the last "unionist" offensive against Jordan. The widely acclaimed tripartite union was never consummated, and within months of the ostensibly historic declaration, relations between the three signatory states had completely broken down. With the dissolution of the first UAR, the abortion of the tripartite union, and Egypt's controversial involvement in the Yemen civil war, it was clear that Nasser had passed his prime and that the Nasserist wave in the region had crested. Doubts about Jordan's viability, however, still persisted. Thus, at the end of this crisis, there remained those in Washington who thought the time had come for serious discussion of how the "future of Jordan could be 'rationalized,'" and whether "there was a 'gambit' [the Western powers] could work out which would be acceptable to all parties, so that Jordan could be de-fused."[42] The emerging consensus, however, was considerably more determined. The voices of the skeptics gradually died down in conjunction with the declining potency of Nasserism, and this time the United States did not hesitate to reassure Hussein while issuing warnings to Egypt, Syria, and Iraq not to imperil his kingdom.[43]

It had now become a Western imperative to forestall Israeli military action in the West Bank along with its unpredictable consequences for Western interests in the region. This meant that the West would have to "ensure by every available means" the continued existence of a regime in Jordan that was not committed to an "Arab crusade" against Israel. If necessary, this should include "increased and open support" of King Hussein.[44] As the British ambassador in Amman summarized the situation at the close of 1963: "The maintenance of Jordan's integrity is an Anglo–American interest," which "at present postulates the survival of the

Hashemite dynasty. . . ." The ambassador concluded, however, that even though "we [Britain and the United States]
pay the piper the tune is often not our calling." King Hussein, he continued, "almost certainly calculates that Britain
and America will bail him out in the last resort since Jordan's
survival is essential to their Middle East policy."[45] That calcu-
lation remained true thereafter and is probably still true today
under 'Abdallah II.

American Support and Israeli Deterrence
Keeping Jordan's Foes at Bay

A major arms deal concluded between Jordan and the United
States in 1965 demonstrated American determination to stand
by Jordan. The deal included the significant upgrading of
Jordan's armed forces with an additional 100 American tanks
and a number of F-104 fighter aircraft and was preceded by
an informal understanding between Israel and Jordan on the
partial demilitarization of the West Bank. According to the
understanding, mediated by the United States, Jordanian armor would not be deployed west of the Jordan River.[46]

Israel's determination to maintain the West Bank as a partially demilitarized security zone also served certain Jordanian
interests with respect to some of its potentially subversive Arab
neighbors. In the mid-1960s, Israel opposed, and thereby
helped Jordan to prevent, the stationing of foreign Arab
armies potentially dangerous to the Hashemite regime on
Jordanian soil. Following the decisions of the first Arab Summit in 1964 to establish a United Arab Command (UAC),
Jordan experienced increasing pressure to permit the deployment in Jordan of Saudi, Iraqi, and Palestine Liberation Army
(PLA) forces. The Jordanians were extremely reluctant to risk
a prolonged stationing of these forces, especially the Iraqis
and the PLA. But since they could hardly express publicly
their fear of subversion by their Arab brethren, deferring the
deployment on the grounds of probable Israeli preemptive
military action proved far more useful. At a secret meeting
between Hussein and Israel's then-foreign minister Golda

Meir in Paris in September 1965, the king suggested that force-ful Israeli public statements against the stationing of foreign Arab armies in Jordan would be helpful.[47]

This tactic served the arguments regularly made at the time in Jordan that the deployment plans of the UAC were not, in principle, objectionable, provided they were put into effect only *after* the Arab armies were fully prepared for all-out war with Israel—which, at the time, they were not—or, alternatively, when it was clear that war was imminent or that hostilities had already begun. In the existing circumstances, Hussein was able to argue, "Israel may exploit the entry of these troops . . . to justify their mounting a major operation," against Jordan. [48] The Egyptian commander of the UAC, Lt. Gen. 'Ali 'Ali 'Amir, tried to no avail to convince the Jordani-ans that if the Arab forces were not pre-positioned well ahead of an outbreak of hostilities, they might be intercepted on their way to the front by Israeli air power. The test of battle proved 'Amir right. On the eve of the June 1967 War, Jordan requested reinforcements from Iraq and Saudi Arabia, but these were prevented by Israeli air strikes from reaching the front on time and had no impact on the outcome of the brief campaign.[49]

The understandings between Israel and Jordan on the partial demilitarization of the West Bank disintegrated on the eve of the war, resulting in Israel's rapid occupation of the West Bank. But even though the situation had changed dra-matically, Jordan's participation in the war did not alter Israel's basic interest in the stability of the relatively moderate Hashemite regime. The West Bank was no longer a poten-tially threatening staging area for an Arab assault on Israel, but the formation of a Syria-dominated northeastern front, stretching across the arc from the Lebanese coast through Syria and Jordan to Aqaba on the Red Sea, remained a major Israeli concern.

In contrast to the early 1960s, after the June War U.S. and Israeli policies were virtually identical in their determination to support the Hashemite Kingdom. Much, though not all, of the doubt and prevarication that had characterized the U.S. position in Nasser's heyday with respect to both Israel and Jordan evaporated in the era following Egypt's humiliating defeat in 1967. The United States seemed thereafter more determined to face down Nasser and his Soviet allies and to vigorously support its own friends in the region.

This new political reality was tested during the Jordanian civil war of September 1970, also known as Black September, when Hussein cracked down on the Palestinian fedayeen who had been launching cross-border raids into Israel from Jordanian territory. After having firmly established a kind of "state within a state" in Jordan, these Palestine Liberation Organization (PLO) armed forces posed the most serious challenge Hussein's regime had ever faced. During the crackdown, some vintage American pessimism and procrastination with regard to Jordan still persisted in bureaucratic corridors. Among the presidential staff, some predicted that the "authority and prestige of the Hashemite regime will continue to decline" and that Hussein faced "an uncertain political future." But this was not the position taken by President Richard Nixon. Henry Kissinger, the president's national security adviser, was of the opinion that Jordan's "collapse would radicalize the entire Middle East. Israel would not acquiesce in the establishment of guerrilla bases all along its Jordanian frontier, and another Middle East war would be extremely likely. Thus, Jordan, in [Kissinger's] view, was a test of [American] capacity to control events in the region." The United States, he argued, could not acquiesce in the forceful destruction of the political balance along the Jordanian front "by dithering on the sidelines, wringing our hands, and then proclaiming our impotence." America, therefore, made it clear that it "attached the greatest importance" to Hussein's survival. It was important, Kissinger explained, "to demonstrate that friendship with the West . . . would be rewarded with effective American support."[50]

In the midst of the crucial campaign against the Palestinian fedayeen, Syrian forces consisting of two armored brigades invaded northern Jordan in support of the Palestinian struggle. Hussein appealed to the United States for support—more specifically, for air strikes (although he did not say by whom)—and the Americans consequently requested that Israel launch the strikes against the Syrian armored incursion in the North. Kissinger put the request to Yitzhak Rabin, Israel's ambassador in Washington at the time, emphasizing American support for the action and recommending that Israel respond accordingly.[51] After having obtained a U.S. commitment to stand firm against the threat of Soviet intervention, the Israelis agreed to assist Jordan and mobilized their reserves. Israeli reinforcements were demonstratively deployed in the northern Jordan Valley; forces on the Golan Heights were reinforced and placed on alert; and Israeli planes flew sorties over the Syrian forces in northern Jordan and also over an Iraqi division that had been deployed in Jordan since 1967 but kept out of the fray. Israel's deputy prime minister, Yigal Allon, declared publicly that the Syrian incursion and the Iraqi division endangered Israeli security interests and that Israel both reserved the right and possessed the military power to protect these interests on its eastern front. The United States issued a strongly worded demand to the Soviet Union that it put pressure on the Syrians to withdraw "without delay," while the Sixth Fleet simultaneously continued the menacing maneuvers it had been carrying out in the eastern Mediterranean since the early days of this crisis.

In the end, the combination of military and diplomatic measures employed by both the United States and Israel restrained the Syrians from either expanding their intervention or activating their air force. Anyway, Israeli involvement proved unnecessary. The Jordanians, emboldened by the promises of external support, managed with their own armor and (rather limited) air power to halt the Syrian advance. This Jordanian military success, coupled with the American-inspired Soviet pressure, forced a Syrian withdrawal. American–Israeli cooperation in the Black September crisis proved not only a turning point in the level of intimacy between the two countries, but also a demonstration of the much-enhanced determination of the United States to guarantee Jordan's stability and staying power.[52]

Notes

1. Zaki Shalom, *David Ben-Gurion: The State of Israel and the Arab World, 1949–1956* (in Hebrew) (Sdeh-Boker: Ben-Gurion University Press, 1995), pp. 208–209.

2. Moshe Zak, *King Hussein Makes Peace: Thirty Years of Secret Talks* (in Hebrew) (Tel Aviv: Begin-Sadat Center for Strategic Studies, Bar Ilan University Press, 1996), p. 37.

3. Ibid., pp. 36–39.

4. Ibid.

5. Uriel Dann, *King Hussein and the Challenge of Arab Radicalism: Jordan, 1955–1967* (New York, Oxford: Oxford University Press, 1989), p. 168.

6. Zak, *King Hussein Makes Peace*, pp. 39–40.

7. Charles Johnston, *The Brink of Jordan* (London: Hamish Hamilton, 1972), p. 66.

8. Ibid., p. 169.

9. Ibid., p. 169.

10. Ibid., p. 125.

11. Dann, *King Hussein*, pp. 168–169.

12. Ibid., pp. 110–111, 169.

13. For information on this meeting, see Zak, *King Hussein Makes Peace*, p. 40; and Dann, *King Hussein*, p. 111.

14. Dann, *King Hussein*, p. 113.

15. National Security Council, "U.S. Policy toward the Near East," November 4, 1958, NSC 5820/1 (Washington: National Archives), pp. 10–12. The author would like to thank Robert Satloff for making a copy of this document available to him.

16. National Intelligence Estimate, "The Outlook for Jordan," March 10, 1959, *FRUS 1958–1960*, vol. 11, *Lebanon and Jordan*, pp. 681–687.

17. Ibid.

18. Memorandum from the Assistant Secretary of State for Near Eastern and South Asian Affairs to the Acting Secretary of State, March 14, 1959, *FRUS 1958–1960*, vol. 11, *Lebanon and Jordan*, pp. 687–690.

19. National Security Council, "U.S. Policy toward the Near East," June 17, 1960, NSC 6011 (National Archives, Washington), as quoted in Zaki Shalom, *The Superpowers, Israel and the Future of Jordan, 1960-1963* (Brighton: Sussex Academic Press, 1999), pp. 132-133.

20. Report from Israeli Embassy Washington to Foreign Ministry Jerusa-

lem, September 15 and October 25, 1960, hetz 3294/19 (Israel State Archives, Jerusalem).

21. Report from Israeli Embassy London to Foreign Ministry Jerusalem, December 22, 1961, hetz 3306/10 (Israel State Archives, Jerusalem).

22. Report from British Embassy Amman to Foreign Office London, March 3, 1962, FO 371/163971, *Records of Jordan (RofJ) 1919–1965*, vol. 13 (1962–1963), (Archive Editions, 1996), p. 64.

23. Report from British Embassy Amman to Foreign Office London, January 9, 1963, FO 371/170263, *RofJ 1919–1965*, vol. 13 (1962–1963), pp. 400–401; and April 24, 1963, FO 371/170278, *RofJ 1919-1965*, vol. 14 (1963–1965), p. 71.

24. Mordechai Gazit, *President Kennedy's Policy toward the Arab States and Israel* (Tel Aviv: Shiloah Center, Tel Aviv University, 1983), p. 22.

25. Report from Foreign Ministry Jerusalem to Israeli Embassy Paris, December 2, 1960, hetz 3340/41 (Israel State Archives, Jerusalem).

26. Report from Israeli Embassy Washington to Foreign Ministry Jerusalem, April 13, 1962, hetz 3378/11; and October 7, 1963, hetz 3378/16 (Israel State Archives, Jerusalem); State Department Memorandum of Conversation between President Kennedy and Golda Meir, December 27, 1962, *FRUS 1961–1963*, vol. 18, *Near East (1962–1963)*, pp. 276–283.

27. Report from US Embassy Amman to Department of State, September 5, 1959, *FRUS 1958–1960*, vol. 11, *Lebanon and Jordan*, p. 729.

28. Ibid., pp. 718–729.

29. Report from Israeli Embassy Washington to Foreign Ministry Jerusalem, April 23, 1962, hetz 3378/13 (Israel State Archives, Jerusalem).

30. Report from British Embassy Amman to Foreign Office London, January 9, 1963, FO 371/170263, *RofJ 1919-1965*, vol. 13 (1962–1963), pp. 391–401.

31. Foreign Office Memorandum, "Her Majesty's Policy towards Jordan," June 14, 1962, FO 371/164096, *RofJ 1919-1965*, vol. 13 (1962–1963), pp. 91, 93.

32. Ibid., p. 91.

33. Dann, *King Hussein*, pp. 127–129; Asher Susser, *On Both Banks of the Jordan: A Political Biography of Wasfi al-Tall* (London: Frank Cass, 1994), pp. 65–68.

34. Zak, *King Hussein Makes Peace*, p. 41.

35. Report from British Embassy Washington to Foreign Office London, April 29, 1963, FO 371/170182, *RofJ 1919-1965*, vol. 14 (1963–1965), pp. 76–79.

36. Dann, *King Hussein*, p. 131.

37. Report from Foreign Office to British Embassy Washington, April 28, 1963, FO 371/170182, *Roff 1919-1965*, vol. 14 (1963–1965), pp. 74–75.

38. Memorandum of the British Consul in Jerusalem, April 26, 1963, FO 371/170182/E1074/12, as quoted in Shalom, *The Superpowers*, p. 84.

39. Memorandum of U.S. Delegation to NATO Alliance within British Foreign Office memorandum, May 2, 1963, FO 371/170182/E1074/9, as quoted in Shalom, *The Superpowers*, p. 163.

40. Zak, *King Hussein Makes Peace*, p. 41; Report from Foreign Ministry Jerusalem to Israeli Embassy Washington, May 5, 1963, hetz 3377/9 (Israel State Archives, Jerusalem).

41. Report from British Consulate Jerusalem to Foreign Office London, March 20, 1963, FO 371/170285, *Roff 1919-1965*, vol. 14 (1963–1965), pp. 10–11; British Foreign Office minute, April 29, 1963, FO 371/170182, *Roff 1919-1965*, vol. 14 (1963–1965), p. 82; Report from British Embassy Tel Aviv to Foreign Office London, April 30, 1963, FO 371/170182, *Roff 1919-1965*, vol. 14 (1963–1965), p. 85; Memorandum of the Director of the Office of Near Eastern Affairs, Department of State, Washington, April 25, 1963, *FRUS 1961–1963*, vol. 18, *Near East (1962–1963)*, pp. 479–481; Telegrams from Department of State Washington to US Embassy Cairo, April 27 and May 27, 1963, *FRUS 1961–1963*, vol. 18, *Near East (1962–1963)*, pp. 488, 556–557; Report from Israeli Embassy Washington to Foreign Ministry Jerusalem, April 30, 1963, hetz 3378/14; Report from Israeli Embassy London to Israeli Embassy Washington, December 2, 1963, hetz 3378/16 (Israel State Archives, Jerusalem).

42. Report from British Embassy Washington to Foreign Office London, May 1, 1963, FO 371/170269/EJ 1015/107, as quoted in the original English in Zaki Shalom, *The Positions of Israel and the Western Powers on the Question of the Future of the Hashemite Kingdom of Jordan in the Early 1960s* (in Hebrew) (forthcoming).

43. Telegram from Department of State Washington to U.S. Embassy Damascus, October 19, 1963, *FRUS 1961–1963*, vol. 18, *Near East (1962–1963)*, pp. 748–749.

44. Report from British Embassy Tel Aviv to Foreign Office London, May 2, 1963, FO 371/170529, *Roff 1919-1965*, vol. 14 (1963–1965), p. 100.

45. Report from British Embassy Amman to Foreign Office London, January 9, 1964, FO 371/175645, *Roff 1919-1965*, vol. 14 (1963–1965), pp. 213–217.

46. Zak, *King Hussein Makes Peace*, pp. 44, 70–71, 75.

47. Ibid., pp. 42, 80.

48. Samir Mutawi, *Jordan in the 1967 War* (Cambridge: Cambridge University Press, 1987), p. 61.

49. Ibid., pp. 59–62; Susser, *On Both Banks of the Jordan*, pp. 76–78.

50. Henry Kissinger, *White House Years* (Boston: Little, Brown and Co., 1979), pp. 596–599, 603, 611.

51. According to Rabin, Kissinger told him that Hussein himself had asked the Americans to relay this request to Israel. See Ibid., p. 623.

52. Ibid., pp. 618–629; Yitzhak Rabin, *Service Record*, vol. 1 (in Hebrew) (Tel Aviv: Ma'ariv, 1979), pp. 311–314; Dan Schueftan, *A Jordanian Option: The 'Yishuv' and the State of Israel vis-à-vis the Hashemite Regime and the Palestinian National Movement* (in Hebrew) (Yad Tabenkin: Hakibbutz Hameuchad Publishing House, 1987), pp. 307–308; Zak, *King Hussein Makes Peace*, p. 45.

Chapter 3

Jordan's Shifting Alliances:
Syria, Iraq, and Saudi Arabia

J ordan's geopolitical centrality has proven to be both an asset and a liability to relations with its more powerful Arab neighbors. Although this centrality has afforded Jordan considerable room to maneuver, it has exposed the kingdom to an ever-present variety of uncomfortable political and economic pressures, as well as resource dependencies (water in particular).[1]

From the very earliest days of the state, Jordan's location compelled its rulers to engage in an endless pursuit of alternating alliances with its various neighbors. King 'Abdallah I, unsatisfied with his modest Trans-Jordanian domain, went so far as to foster a lifelong ambition to unite Greater Syria under his crown. Although it was a futile pursuit, he never abandoned this dream to his dying day, even as the Iraqi branch of the Hashemite family was concurrently promoting its own scheme for Fertile Crescent unity. Despite this internecine competition, the Hashemite monarchies of Iraq and Jordan were usually allied together against just about everyone else in the era of Arab dynastic politics, or until the early 1950s. The Egyptian and Saudi monarchies, for their part, aligned themselves with republican Syria and Christian-dominated Lebanon against Hashemite expansionist ambition. But the overthrow of the monarchies in the leading Arab states of Egypt (1952) and Iraq (1958) revolutionized inter-Arab politics, and the stage was set for an entirely new array of alternating alliances founded on geopolitical, strategic, economic, and ideological interests. This would be a new era of Arab radicalism in which the young and often beleaguered King Hussein could hardly afford the luxury of expansionist designs. All his energies were devoted to preserving his own regime.

'The Monarchs' Trade Union'

The origins of the Saudi–Hashemite conflict can be traced to the early eighteenth-century struggle between the two dynasties over the Hijaz and its holy places in Mecca and Medina—a contest the Hashemites lost when the Saudis finally ousted them from Mecca in 1925. 'Abdallah never forgave the Saudis for this, and furthermore, 'Abd al-'Aziz (Ibn Sa'ud) suspected the Hashemites of retaining the ambition to restore their former realm.

In the early 1950s, however, both 'Abdallah and 'Abd al-'Aziz passed from the scene, and by the middle part of the decade, the regional environment had created a whole new set of interests. The challenge of Nasser was growing as his popularity soared throughout the Arab world. Egypt's nationalization of the Suez Canal in 1956, the ensuing Suez War, and the formation of the UAR in early 1958 had established him as the unchallenged Arab leader—a development which propelled the Saudis and the Hashemites toward historical reconciliation. By the height of Jordan's domestic crisis in April 1957, when an Egyptian-backed Syrian invasion was a distinct possibility, public Saudi support for Jordan proved both timely and helpful.[2] Not long afterward, when the Iraqi Hashemites were overthrown in July 1958, Jordan and Saudi Arabia would become increasingly dependent on each other for what both regarded as their political survival.[3]

In effect, these two dynastic enemies became allies as they created a royalist–conservative coalition, aptly named the "Monarchs' Trade Union," to face the onslaught of anti-Western and anti-monarchist revolutionaries. Indeed, as Laurie Brand explains, "Jordan had come to constitute a security belt for the Saudis, and it continued to serve as a buffer between the conservative peninsular states and the various revolutionary, or pan-Arab, political currents that swept through the Arab East in successive decades."[4] Jordan also acted as a buffer for the Saudis against the Arab–Israeli conflict, while by the early 1970s, Saudi assistance had become the "cornerstone of Jordan's budget security."[5] Indeed, aid from the Saudis helped the kingdom to underwrite assistance for arms purchases, domestic security, and subsidized oil supplies, as "a stable Jordan was viewed as a key to Saudi security as well."[6] The Jordanians, for their part, provided the Saudis with a variety of military and intelligence services. Between 1972 and 1982, Jordan seconded more than two thousand officers and troops to the Gulf states and trained a similar number of Saudi officers and troops on Jordanian soil. Saudi Arabia also became one of Jordan's main trading partners and a major employer of Jordanian labor.[7] Indeed, until the Gulf War of 1990–91, Jordan's relations with Saudi Arabia were more consistently secure, stable, and amicable than they were with any of its other neighbors.

The Surprising Resilience of Jordanian–Iraqi Relations

The Nasserist challenge did more than encourage the Jordanians and the Saudis to let bygones be bygones. The union between Egypt and Syria—the United Arab Republic (UAR), formed in February 1958 when Nasser was at the peak of his regional influence—also propelled the Hashemites in Jordan and Iraq into a hastily constructed defensive federation of their own against the anti-monarchist revolutionary republics. The federation, however, was short lived. In July 1958, the Hashemites in Iraq were overthrown and brutally murdered in a military coup led by 'Abd al-Karim Qasim, and Hussein now faced what appeared to be complete encirclement by like-minded radical regimes. It soon became clear, however, that Qasim would not submit to Nasser's lead, and within months relations between Iraq and the UAR had degenerated to the point of no return, "even worse than they had been in the days of the old regime."[8] Less than two years after the removal of the Hashemite regime in Iraq, Jordan renewed its diplomatic relations with Iraq, and the kingdom's room to maneuver was not abridged to the extent initially expected. In fact, Jordan escaped isolation as the two states closed ranks in the face of UAR sabotage and subversion.

Although relations with Iraq were hardly ideal during this period, they rarely deteriorated to the level of vitriolic and subversive hostility that pervaded those between Hashemite Jordan and Ba'thi Syria for much of the 1960s. Nor were relations with the Ba'thi regime that came to power in Iraq in 1968 marked by unmitigated hostility or relentless efforts to subvert the monarchy in Jordan.[9] Despite the revolution in Iraq, a residue of familiarity remained, and Hussein still seemed to feel more at ease in Baghdad than in either Damascus or Riyadh.[10] During the 1967 war, for example, when the kingdom's relations with Syria were still overtly hostile, Jordan welcomed an Iraqi division to shore up its front with Israel. The Iraqi forces remained in Jordan for nearly four years and, most importantly, refrained from any involvement in Jordan's civil war in 1970— when their fellow Ba'this in Damascus launched an invasion into the kingdom on behalf of the Palestinian fedayeen.

Ideologically embarrassed by their own pragmatic passivity, however, the Iraqis embarked on a sustained propaganda campaign against Jordan soon after the civil war. Relations consequently soured, and the Iraqis were asked to withdraw their contingent from Jordan; they did so without much ado.[11] In mid-1971, after the final expulsion of the fedayeen by the Jordanians, Iraq joined Syria in closing its borders with Jordan. The Iraqis soon relented, while the Syrian closure, which began in 1970, was more persistent and damaging to the kingdom and lasted until 1973. Jordan was dependent on access through Syria to Mediterranean ports (acutely between 1967 and 1975 when the alternative Suez route was closed), and the Syrians rarely hesitated to deny Jordan passage by closing the border whenever they wished to register their political displeasure.[12]

Iraqi–Syrian Rivalry and Jordan's Expanded Room to Maneuver

Jordan's relations with neighbors like Syria and Iraq were hardly stable. But the fact that Syria and Iraq were almost constantly at loggerheads with each other tended to expand the kingdom's room to maneuver in the Fertile Crescent. Jordan, therefore, benefited from the longstanding rivalry between Syria and Iraq, further exacerbated by competition between the Baʻthi regimes in both countries as they jockeyed for regional supremacy. When Jordan's relations declined with one, they invariably improved with the other, allowing the kingdom to address not only its strategic interests, but also its constant quest for financial and economic security, an essential prerequisite of domestic stability.

As a *terra media* poised along Israel's longest front and situated at the geographic and demographic core of the Palestinian question, Jordan was potentially both an asset and a liability for the Syrians. Whether in preparation for war or for peace, the Hashemite regime could be valuable if convinced or coerced into behaving in conformity with Syrian interests. But this was rarely achieved, and more often than not, Jordanian policy toward Israel and the Palestinians became a bone of contention between Jordan and Syria.

In any case, generally and historically speaking, relations with Iraq were a more attractive prospect for Jordan than a relationship of dependence on Syria. Ever since the mid-1950s, having aligned itself with Nasser, Syria had been and remained an object of suspicion for the Hashemites. Indeed, Jordan had good cause to fear Syrian subversion, which took the form of sabotage operations in the kingdom, political assassination, and worse.[13] But when Jordan's relations cooled with Iraq in the early 1970s, they also gradually improved with Syria. The Syrians restored diplomatic ties with Jordan shortly before the October War, probably in a bid to prepare for the resumption of armed conflict with Israel. During the war itself, Jordan dispatched two armored brigades to assist the Syrians in the fighting on the Golan; when the war ended, relations continued to improve as the two countries forged an alliance of sorts, in which enhanced military coordination featured prominently.

The Syrians were particularly concerned about the potential exploitation by Israel of Jordanian territory or air space as an indirect approach to Syria, thus outflanking the Golan defenses from the south. At the same time, both countries were apprehensive about Egypt's advances toward a separate peace with Israel, foreshadowed by the signing of a second disengagement agreement with the latter in September 1975. Both Syria and Jordan also had an interest in joining forces to "persuade" the Gulf states to make good on their as-yet-unfulfilled promises of aid. Furthermore, Jordan had suffered intensely from the Syrian border closure in 1970–71 as a state dependent on transit trade. The kingdom was now keenly interested in securing a level of economic cooperation with the Syrians that would make them think twice before resorting to such a severe punitive action again.[14]

In the mid-1970s there was much talk in political and media circles, as well as some symbolic action, of advancing a process of "integration" (*takamul*) between Syria and Jordan. The Jordanians were, however, extremely wary of being overwhelmed by their northern neighbor and kept the Syrians at arms' length throughout the brief honeymoon period. Whereas the Syrians were most interested in establishing an effective eastern front against Israel, Jordan was more concerned with finding a place in a reactivated Middle East peace process. Their differences were far too substantive for the relationship to last, and the Sadat initiative of 1977 not only split the alliance, but nearly drove Syria and Jordan into armed confrontation at the end of 1980. The Syrians suspected that Hussein sought the role of a "second Sadat," looking for an opening to complement "the Camp David plot," and they consequently continued to threaten Jordan with force in later years to prevent such a scenario from emerging on their border.[15]

In the meantime, Jordan's brief alliance with Syria had caused relations with Iraq to deteriorate. Although Jordanian–Iraqi trade links were maintained on an even keel and the two countries benefited from Iraq's use of the port of Aqaba, the Iraqis nevertheless registered their displeasure with the alliance through intimidation. In November 1976, a hotel in Amman was attacked by terrorists whom the Jordanians accused of having been trained in Iraq "with the knowledge and under the supervision of the Iraqi authorities."[16] Despite this charge, Jordan avoided a rift with Iraq, for as good as relations with Syria may have been at the time, the kingdom was disinclined to burn its bridges with Baghdad. Consequently, when Syrian–Jordanian relations returned to their more hostile norm, the way was paved for the Jordanian–Iraqi alliance of the 1980s to emerge, wherein Ba'thist Iraq and Hashemite Jordan were to enjoy "much closer and much more cordial relations than they had when both were Hashemite monarchies."[17]

Notes

1. Arnon Sofer, "Jordan Facing the 1990s: Location, Metropolis, and Water," in Joseph Nevo and Ilan Pappe, eds., *Jordan in the Middle East, 1948–1988: The Making of a Pivotal State* (London: Frank Cass, 1994), pp. 32–35.

2. Elie Podeh, "Ending an Age-Old Rivalry: The *Rapprochement* between the Hashemites and the Saudis, 1956–58," in Asher Susser and Aryeh Shmuelevitz, eds., *The Hashemites in the Modern Arab World: Essays in Honour of the Late Professor Uriel Dann* (London: Frank Cass, 1995), pp. 85–108; Joseph Nevo, "Jordan and Saudi Arabia: The Last Royalists," in Nevo and Pappe, eds., *Jordan in the Middle East, 1948–1988*, pp. 103–118; Uriel Dann, *King Hussein and the Challenge of Arab Radicalism: Jordan, 1955–1967* (New York, Oxford: Oxford University Press, 1989), p. 65.

3. Podeh, "Ending an Age-Old Rivalry," pp. 85–108; Nevo, "Jordan and Saudi Arabia," pp. 103–118.

4. Laurie Brand, *Jordan's Inter-Arab Relations: The Political Economy of Alliance Making* (New York: Columbia University Press, 1994), p. 88. This work is an excellent, though somewhat overstated, analysis of the quest for economic or budgetary security as a determinant of Jordan's foreign policy.

5. Ibid., p. 105.

6. Ibid., p. 88.

7. Ibid., pp. 88, 93, 96–97, 105; Nevo, "Jordan and Saudi Arabia," p. 111.

8. Malcolm Kerr, *The Arab Cold War: Gamal Abd al-Nasir and His Rivals, 1958–1970* (London: Oxford University Press, 1971), p. 17.

9. Amatzia Baram, "Baathi Iraq and Hashimite Jordan: From Hostility to Alignment," *Middle East Journal* 45, no. 1 (Winter 1991), p. 52.

10. Joseph Nevo, "Jordan's Relations with Iraq: Ally or Victim?" in Amatzia Baram and Barry Rubin, eds., *Iraq's Road to War* (New York: St. Martin's Press, 1994), p. 136.

11. Ibid., p. 53.

12. Joseph Nevo, "Syria and Jordan: The Politics of Subversion," in Moshe Ma'oz and Avner Yaniv, eds., *Syria Under Assad: Domestic Constraints and Regional Risks* (New York: St. Martin's Press, 1986), p. 150.

13. Amatzia Baram, "Baathi Iraq and Hashimite Jordan: From Hostility to Alignment," *Middle East Journal* 45, no. 1 (Winter 1991), p. 55; Nevo, "Jordan's Relations with Iraq," p. 145; Brand, p. 198; Uriel Dann, *King Hussein's Strategy of Survival,* Policy Papers, no. 29 (Washington: The Washington Institute for Near East Policy, 1992), pp. 43–44, 54.

14. Brand, pp. 154–155, 158–159, 165; Moshe Ma'oz, "Jordan in Asad's Greater Syria Strategy," in Nevo and Pappe, eds., *Jordan in the Middle East, 1948–1988,* pp. 97–98.

15. Asher Susser, "Jordan," in *Middle East Contemporary Survey (MECS),* vol. I (1976–77), pp. 484–485; vol. II (1977–78), pp. 590–591; vol. V (1980–81), pp. 650–651; vol. VII (1982–83), p. 644.

16. Susser, "Jordan," *MECS,* vol. I (1976–77), p. 487.

17. Nevo, "Jordan's Relations with Iraq," p. 146.

Chapter 4

Jordan, the Gulf War, and the Rupture of Traditional Alliances

Iraq, with its own wealth and huge potential market for Jordanian goods, appeared far more promising economically to Jordan than did Syria, and it was also less of a political burden. Because Iraq (unlike Syria) was not a frontline state and was, therefore, less immediately implicated in Arab–Israeli issues, differences with respect to Israel were less likely to irritate the relationship. For Iraq, the added benefit of prying Jordan away from Syria could only be seen as a net gain.

Once Jordan had made up its mind not to join the Camp David process, it was quite willing to follow the Iraqi lead in opposition to the Israeli–Egyptian accords, especially when enticed by attractive offers of Arab financial aid orchestrated by the Iraqis. (Jordan's Saudi allies had also shown concern about the kingdom's warmer relations with Syria, and they had held back financial aid as an expression of disapproval.[1]) It was, however, the rise to power of Saddam Husayn in Iraq in 1979 that became the turning point in Jordan–Iraq relations.

Jordan's Alliance with Saddam Husayn's Iraq

Although he had been the real power behind the presidency for years, Saddam's formal assumption of supreme authority coincided with Iraq's projected image of a powerful, self-confident, and ambitious state.[2] It was deemed expedient that Jordan seek and maintain the friendship of this rising power of the Fertile Crescent, particularly in the face of a rapid and unsettling succession of political changes in the region that were effecting the kingdom, compounding Jordanian unease: Egypt had departed from the fold of Arab states in confrontation with Israel; the shah had been overthrown in the Iranian revolution; relations with Syria had deteriorated; and Israel had elected a new right-wing government.

An added benefit for the Jordanians was the fact that the Saudis were much more comfortable with Jordan's relationship with the Iraqis in the 1980s than they had ever been with the Jordanian–Syrian relationship in the previous decade. Ayatollah Ruhollah Khomeini's Iran—religious and anti-Ba'thi on the one hand; revolutionary, anti-Western, and anti-monarchist on the other—gave all three states common cause to unite against this new threat from the East.[3] Their common cause, however, meant Syria's relative isolation (except for its own rather "un-Ba'thi" alliance with the Islamic Republic in Iran).

Jordan was completely aligned with Iraq from the very onset of Baghdad's conflict with Tehran, even before the actual outbreak of war in the summer of 1980. Iraq, from the Jordanian geopolitical viewpoint, both provided a bulwark against Iran's ambition "to export the revolution to its neighbors," and created "strategic depth" vis-à-vis Israel.[4] As King Hussein often suggested at the time, Jordan's consistent support for the Iraqis in their contest with Iran placed Iraq under an obligation to respond in kind in the event of a conflict with Israel. The Arabs, he declared, could "not allow any aggression against any part of the Arab homeland from whatever source."[5] And there was furthermore no justification for distinguishing between "these two [Iranian and Zionist] aggressions against the Arab nation."[6] After the war with Iran and shortly before Saddam's Kuwaiti adventure, Iraq did make it clear that it would come to the aid of any Arab state attacked by Israel. Moreover, Iraq now seemed inclined to offer legitimizing gestures of goodwill to the Hashemite regime, indicating to the Palestine Liberation Organization (PLO) leadership, for example, that the continued existence of the monarchy in Jordan was an Iraqi interest. Concurrently, "Iraqi politicians spared no effort in stressing their country's new approach . . . whereby 'interference in the internal affairs of others [did] not make one a pan-Arabist.'"[7]

Jordan's relations with Syria had anyway begun to sour before the cementing of the kingdom's alliance with Iraq, and matters progressively worsened thereafter. The price the Jordanians had to pay for their alignment with Iraq was exacted in the form of Syrian subversion. In the early 1980s, the Jordanians were accusing the "fascist sectarian regime in Syria" of having perpetrated attacks on their diplomats in various countries, for bomb attacks in Amman, and even for attempting to assassinate Jordanian prime minister Mudar Badran in 1981. Syrian officials, for their part, called for the "overthrow of the Jordanian regime—with its king, tools, figureheads and agent forces,"[8] repeatedly accusing the Jordanians of aiding and abetting the Muslim Brotherhood in Syria in its struggle against the Ba'thi regime. There was apparently some substance to the Syrian allegations. During one occasional lull in Jordanian–Syrian antagonism in late 1985, Hussein even admitted as much in an extraordinary public confession, in which he claimed to have to have "suddenly" discovered that "some of those who had something to do with . . . bloody acts [in Syria] were among us."[9]

Meanwhile Iraq, having been denied the use of its own ports during the war with Iran, developed an unprecedented dependence on Jordan and its invaluable lifeline from the port of Aqaba. The port had become more important to Iraq with the reopening of the Suez Canal in 1975, and given Jordan's traditional involvement in transit trade, the kingdom was more than willing to expand its highway and port system—with Iraqi aid—to accommodate Iraqi needs.[10] From the early 1980s, the Iraqis invested heavily in the Jordanian transport industry, the kingdom's highway system, and the expansion of the absorptive capacity of the Aqaba port.[11] At the same time, as Jordan's economy was increasingly geared to serve Iraqi demands, Jordan began to import part of its oil supply from Iraq in exchange for the goods and services for which Baghdad was having difficulty paying as the war dragged on.

Jordan and Iraq's economic and strategic codependence was consequently a mixed blessing. On the one hand, the end of the Iran–Iraq War finally relieved Jordan of its fears of Iranian revolutionary expansionism. Moreover, Iraqi military power could now be seen as an effective deterrent against Israel, and increasing manifestations of Jordanian military cooperation with Iraq began to appear. On the other hand, the war's end meant Iraq's reduced dependence on Jordan, coupled with Iraq's potential to develop into an intimidating regional superpower aspiring to regional domination. Accordingly, the Jordanians had no intention of allowing the permanent deployment of Iraqi troops on their soil (this could also have had the undesirable consequence of provoking Israel). Jordan, pronounced King Hussein, intended to build up its own military force capable of absorbing the first blow (from an Israeli attack), providing other Arab states time to send reinforcements to the Jordanian front.[12]

The Jordanians also hoped that eventual Iraqi rehabilitation and reconstruction would pave the way for new outlets for their manpower, more exports to Iraq, and investment by Iraq in Jordan, not to mention repayment of the large Iraqi debt to Jordan accumulated during the war. In early 1989, Jordan joined Iraq, Egypt, and North Yemen in the formation of the Arab Cooperation Council (ACC), in the hopes that the organization (especially Iraq) would provide an expanded market for Jordanian exports, jobs for Jordan's unemployed skilled workers, and business opportunities for the private sector. But the countries of the ACC were most predominantly united in debt. (Nothing much came of the council, as it was torn asunder by the Iraqi invasion of Kuwait in August 1990—dashing any remaining economic and political expectations Jordan had from its ties to Iraq.) Transit traffic from Aqaba to Iraq had also sharply declined with the end of the Iran–Iraq War, bringing a further and immediate negative effect to bear on the Jordanian economy. Riots rocked the south of the country in April 1989, sparked in part by breadwinners in the transport and trucking industry suffering the consequences of the reduced traffic. By the end of the decade, Jordan's economy, which had been in decline since the mid-1980s—the result of multiple causes including the Iraqi impact—plunged into crisis.[13]

Yet, even though Jordan had reason to be disappointed by the unrealized economic benefits of its association with Iraq, the kingdom's gravitation into the Iraqi orbit continued unabated. Jordanians probably still hoped to retrieve their debt as, in the first half of 1990, nearly a quarter of Jordan's total exports were destined for Iraq and 75 percent of the kingdom's industrial establishments were manufacturing primarily for the Iraqi market.[14] Indeed, Jordan had a healthy respect for, and fear of, Iraq's power and regional ambition. Yet, bearing Jordan's geopolitical constraints in mind, King Hussein believed that there was "nothing harder than isolation,"[15] and Iraq was serving as an effective counterweight to Syria, as well as a deterrent to Israel. An editorial in the *Jordan Times* in early 1990 noted that the Jordanian–Iraqi relationship was a "clear signal to all those forces that entertain hostile intentions . . . that Jordan does not stand alone. . . . Both friend and foe must now reckon with Iraq's new strength."[16]

The Jordanian leadership had reservations about Iraqi bellicosity toward Israel, fearing a conflagration that could embroil the kingdom as well. Nevertheless, they increasingly allowed themselves to be drawn into the propaganda war, consistently coming to Iraq's defense when the latter was engaged in a confrontation with international public opinion. For example, when Saddam accused the West of seeking to prevent the Arab nation from "making progress and building up its strength," the Jordanian media, at times verging on the euphoric, applauded this kind of "unequivocal Iraqi position" that had revived the hope of the Arabs to retrieve their "nation's past glories."[17]

Indeed, for the Jordanians, Iraq was not only a strategic ally deterring Jordan's other neighbors, but also the potential powerhouse for restructuring the Arab economic and political order. According to King Hussein's vision, this new economic order was to be founded on a more equitable distribution of wealth between the Arab states, while the political order was to be based on a cohesive bloc of states that would control Arab resources. This, in turn, would allow the Arabs to form a more balanced relationship with the United States and a united Europe, especially in a post–Cold War era wherein the Soviet counterweight to the United States no longer existed. Iraq was essential to this vision as the pivot of the power structure creating the new Arab order, preventing the Middle East from falling under the total hegemony of a United States biased in favor of Israel.

In keeping with this vision, the Jordanians surmised that even if Iraq would never be a major source of crucial economic aid for the kingdom, the Iraqis could at least ensure that other Arab states in the region would be, thereby rescuing Jordan once and for all from its economic troubles and sparing King Hussein the periodic humiliation of begging for the financial welfare of his country. Years before the outbreak of the crisis between Iraq and Kuwait, Prince Hassan contended that the inequality in income and wealth between the various Arab countries was "a cause of resentment, recrimination, instability, and discord in the region." This resentment, he explained, was fomented by the fact that the "non-oil-producing countries [were] not adequately compensated for the contribution that they [made] to the oil-producing countries through the educated and technically skilled manpower that they export to them."[18] When the kingdom plunged into economic crisis at the end of the decade, Jordanians did not hesitate to lay the blame for their hardship on the failure of the wealthy Arab states—Saudi Arabia excluded—to honor their pledges of aid.

In February 1990, Hassan called for an Arab summit to address the "economic disparities between the wealthy oil-producing countries in the Gulf and those, like Jordan, which exported labor to them." At the Arab summit convened in May of that year, Jordan firmly supported Iraq's case against Kuwait on oil pricing. When the crisis between Iraq and Kuwait finally broke in July with Saddam Husayn championing the Arab "have-nots," the Jordanian media uniformly supported the Iraqi demand for fairer interstate distribution of Arab oil wealth. Those who had "departed from the nation" were now urged to consider "how different matters could have been if the billions of dollars squandered because of their selfish pricing policy had been used to pay off the debts of the poorer Arab states."[19]

Jordan, Iraq, and the Gulf War

The Jordanians did not, however, support the use of force to solve the oil-pricing problem, and Iraq's invasion and annexation of Kuwait was more than they had bargained for. After some brief hesitation, Jordan announced that it would not recognize the provisional government established by the Iraqis in Kuwait, calling the annexation "totally unacceptable." The Jordanians further believed that the solution to the crisis ought to be found in Iraqi withdrawal, reinstatement of the Kuwaiti ruling family, and negotiations within an Arab framework to resolve the dispute. But at the same time, Jordan refused to join the majority of Arab states in condemning Iraq, and although the Jordanians expressed their support for unconditional Iraqi withdrawal, their actual position was far more ambiguous. Jordan showed considerable understanding and sympathy for Saddam Husayn, suggesting that Iraq did in fact have legitimate grievances against Kuwait. Both King Hussein and Prince Hassan explained that Iraq could hardly be expected to simply "go back to square one" without some outline of an agreement with Kuwait over their border dispute. Total and unconditional Iraqi withdrawal, Hassan explained, would be tantamount to "complete surrender."[20]

Jordan's apologetics on behalf of Iraq and the inherent ambiguities of the kingdom's position were the result of an ongoing, but virtually hopeless, effort to reconcile conflicting domestic, Arab, and international pressures and interests. In some important respects, King Hussein and his people genuinely identified with Iraq. But it was also as patently clear to the king as to anyone else that there was a steep price to pay for supporting Iraq against the wishes of Jordan's traditional allies in the West and the Arab world. True, the price for opposing Iraq might have been equally, or even more, painful; Jordan's alliance with Iraq was, after all, not only born out of shared economic and strategic interests, but also out of fear of Iraqi power. Still, whereas Jordan chose not to oppose Iraq, the Hashemites could hardly have condoned the devouring of a neighboring state and the forceful overthrow of a monarchy in order to rectify perceived colonial injustices. The Jordanian monarchy, as an artificial colonialist creation, had itself once been on the receiving end of pan-Arab denunciation. In a glass house of its own, the kingdom was therefore hardly in a position to cast the first stone.

Saddam Husayn's immense popularity among the Jordanian populace further complicated Jordanian policymaking. By defying Western powers, Saddam had instantly become a hero to the masses, and this popular sentiment certainly influenced the king's decision to continue supporting Iraq. As Prince Hassan acknowledged, Saddam Husayn's popularity in the kingdom was a "limiting factor on Jordan's maneuverability."[21]

Yet another reason for Jordan's tilt toward Iraq was King Hussein's extreme sensitivity to his own image—and that of the Hashemites in general—before the proponents of pan-Arabism and of Arab historiography. In the past, the Hashemites had been the object of Arab nationalist opprobrium for their seeming conciliatory posture toward British imperialism and Zionism. This troubled Hussein, who desperately hoped to correct the record. Throughout his reign, the king consciously sought whenever possible to adopt positions that would conform to the patriotic pan-Arab consensus. With Saddam Husayn emerging as the standard-bearer of popular pan-Arabism against the "new crusaders," the pressure on Hussein to fulfill popular expectations was in many ways a repetition of his predicament during the Baghdad Pact crisis in 1955 and yet again during the fateful days of June 1967.[22]

Jordan therefore opposed the deployment of foreign forces in Saudi Arabia from the outset and accordingly refused to join the coalition poised against Iraq. The king and crown prince repeatedly expressed their anxieties about a military rather than a diplomatic solution to the dispute, fearing a war that would involve Iraq and Israel and turn the kingdom into a "killing ground" crushed between its two powerful neighbors.[23] Moreover, Jordan had no interest in a conflict that would lead to the destruction of the Iraqi military machine on which they themselves relied as a deterrent. King Hussein even warned against a settlement that would strip Iraq of its military and technological power, thus giving Israel the upper hand in the region. This, he contended, would undermine the prospects for a solution to the Palestinian problem.[24]

Hussein probably assumed that should it became necessary, Jordan's traditional allies—the major Western powers, Saudi Arabia, and the other Gulf states—would forgive this aberrance and "bail him out" just as the British ambassador had predicted nearly thirty years earlier. In any event, the king may have thought, Arab moderates and conservatives, the Western powers, and even Israel would prefer Hashemite order to chaos in Jordan.[25] But Jordan's refusal to join the anti-Iraqi coalition, its unwillingness even to condemn Iraq, and its apologetics on Saddam's behalf all aroused the fury and suspicion of Jordan's usual friends. This was true of its more or less consistent financial supporters in Saudi Arabia and the Gulf, Egypt, and, most important, the United States.[26]

As furious as Jordan's friends may have been, it should also be borne in mind that at the time of the Kuwaiti crisis, the Jordanian leadership felt increasingly let down, both politically and economically, by its traditional allies. By the late 1980s, Jordan had become rather resentful toward many of the Arab states, particularly in the aftermath of the Algiers Summit of June 1988, where Hussein had failed to earn the recognition and respect of his Arab brethren for the Hashemites' historical role in Palestine. Moreover, some of the kingdom's financial supporters in the Gulf had not only failed to fulfill their ten-year financial pledges made at the Baghdad Summit of 1978, but had even declined to extend emergency aid to Jordan when it plunged into economic crisis at the end of the 1980s. Similarly, the Jordanians were deeply disappointed in the United States for having failed to pressure Israel to adhere to a "land for peace" formula while still expecting Jordan to deliver the Palestinians. Having been let down during their times of need, the Jordanians hardly felt bound in the 1990–91 crisis to rush to the side of those who had so recently failed them.[27]

The Price of Isolation

Before the Gulf War, Saudi Arabia was Jordan's most reliable source of financial support in the Arab world. It was the only Arab state to regularly fulfill its annual commitment ($300 million) to Jordan for the full ten years agreed upon at the 1978 Arab summit held in Baghdad.[28] But by the end of the 1980s, Saudi aid had begun to wane, possibly contributing toward Jordanian readiness to risk its ties with a less wealthy Saudi Arabia.[29] The Saudis, for their part, conjured up the specter of historical Hashemite ambition, suspecting the ultimate conspiracy—that the Jordanians were colluding with Iraq to redivide the Arabian Peninsula and reclaim the Hijaz and its holy places for themselves. Feeling betrayed, the Saudis recalled their ambassador from Amman on October 6, 1990, having already resorted to a variety of economic and other punitive measures, including the cessation of all oil supplies to Jordan as of September 19.[30]

Hussein's isolation was anything but "splendid." The U.S. Congress conveyed an "unmistakable sign of its displeasure" by withholding a commitment of aid to Jordan for fiscal year 1990–91, and Jordan's relations with Washington plunged to an all-time low.[31] When Allied air strikes on Iraq began in mid-January 1991, the Jordanian official media denounced what they saw as a "brutal onslaught against an Arab and Muslim people." Jordanian appeals for a ceasefire were ignored as popular fury and indignation mounted in the kingdom against the continued bombardment of Iraq. Jordanian fears of being drawn into the conflict were similarly exacerbated by the possibility of Israeli retaliation against Iraq for the Scud missile attacks on its cities, and on February 6 a desperate and frustrated King Hussein launched an unprecedented verbal assault on the United States. In a speech to the nation, both representing and setting the tone for popular anti-American sentiment, the king denounced the "all-out ferocious war [that had been] imposed on fraternal Iraq." Without as much as mentioning Iraqi responsibility for the crisis, he accused the United States and its allies of seeking "to destroy Iraq and to rearrange the regional state of affairs." The speech, needless to say, was not well received in Washington. Hussein was forced to backtrack somewhat, clarifying that any previous omission of Iraqi responsibility was only because he had already mentioned it "zillions of times before." Jordan, he noted, had always been opposed to the occupation of territory by war, and this applied to the Kuwaiti case as well. Prince Hassan, for his part, asserted reassuringly that Kuwaiti sovereignty was "beyond dispute," but his statements were nevertheless embellished with understanding overtures to Iraq, noting, for example, that Iraqi territorial claims on some Kuwaiti territory were "not without foundation." Such statements could hardly have been helpful to Jordan's already troubled relations with the United States and the Gulf countries.[32]

The Gulf War aggravated Jordan's already serious economic crisis, as trade with Iraq was severely curtailed by the imposition of international sanctions. Operation of the Aqaba port was disrupted by the allied blockade, and the return of some 250,000 Jordanian citizens (mostly Palestinian) from Kuwait placed immediate and further strains on the country's infrastructure and general economy (although it did provide for a temporary mini-boom shortly thereafter). After all, "the mother of all economic problems" faced by Jordan was the imbalance between population and resources.[33] Facing such an economic predicament precisely when the kingdom's relations with its traditional supporters had been so severely disrupted provided material for renewed predictions of gloom and doom.

The Fortunes of Geopolitical Centrality

But the pessimistic and much-anticipated economic collapse did not, in the end, occur. Apparently the Jordanian government, accustomed to exploiting the interests of external powers for the sake of the kingdom's stability, had deliberately exaggerated the losses it expected to incur as a direct result of the Gulf crisis. This had its desired effect and produced more than enough emergency foreign aid to forestall the collapse of the fragile Jordanian economy. Although Jordan's traditional allies in the United States, Saudi Arabia, and the Gulf were certainly in no mood to bail Jordan out, others were. Japan provided Jordan with a soft loan of $450 million, following on a similar loan of $250 million made in 1990. In fact, in the aftermath of the 1990–91 Gulf crisis, Japan became the single most important provider of foreign aid to Jordan (the kingdom received another $441 million in Japanese aid in 1995).[34] Germany also offered a grant of DM150 million ($95 million), in addition to a similar grant of DM180 million ($ 115 million) it had made in 1990, making Jordan the highest per capita recipient of German aid (DM2 billion [$ 1.3 billion] since the early 1960s).

Both Japanese and German officials explained their largesse in terms of Jordan's importance both to regional stability and to an eventual resolution of the Palestinian problem. According to Prince Hassan, Japan acknowledged Jordan's "pivotal role in regional security and stability" in the "resource rich region" of the Middle East.[35] One Jordanian analyst credited Japan's interest in supporting Jordan not only to American blessing for Japanese intervention, but also to Japan's recognition of Jordan as a stabilizing force in a region of crucial importance to a major importer of Middle East oil.[36] At the same time, the European Community provided Jordan with grants worth $210 million to compensate for losses incurred while adhering to the sanctions against Iraq.[37] By May 1991, Jordan had reportedly received emergency assistance totaling some $1.1 billion in soft loans and grants. Foreign currency reserves in 1991 actually reached their highest level ever ($878 million).[38] Moreover, Jordan's implementation of the 1989 International Monetary Fund (IMF) restructuring plan made it eligible for foreign debt rescheduling and for further and substantial international economic assistance through the IMF and World Bank.[39]

Jordan's Shift Away from Iraq

Militarily defeated and under the pressure of international sanctions, Iraq was no longer the regional powerhouse, strategic hinterland, nor ideal trading partner that Jordan had previously envisioned. Although Jordan was now receiving all its oil supplies from post–Gulf War Iraq, essentially at no real cost (the oil was supplied at concessionary rates for the repayment of Iraq's outstanding debt to Jordan), Saddam's recklessness had transformed Iraq into more of a liability than an asset. In fact, Jordan's gradual but consistent shift away from Iraq was already discernible in late February 1991 when it became increasingly apparent that the latter faced certain defeat. An early expression of Jordan's frustration with Saddam's intransigence was Hussein's acceptance of a Soviet initiative for an Iraqi withdrawal from Kuwait to end the war, even though both Jordan and Iraq had previously insisted that the initiative must include linkage to the Palestinian issue.[40]

As Jordan sought to improve its ties with both the United States and the Gulf states, its position toward Iraq became ever more ambiguous. On the one hand, Jordanian public opinion, as reflected in the press and in parliament, remained staunchly supportive of Iraq in its continuing confrontation with the United States and its allies. King Hussein and Prince Hassan, who were concerned about the regional influence and ambition of Iran, repeatedly expressed their support for Iraq's territorial integrity. Because of the implications for Iraq, and by extension for Jordan as well, Jordan had reservations about the U.S. policy of dual containment, which was enunciated formally in May 1993. Jordan also consistently advocated the removal of sanctions

against Iraq, which would provide for the much-needed resumption of unfettered Jordanian trade with the potentially
large and lucrative Iraqi market.

On the other hand, Hussein became increasingly frustrated by Saddam's intransigence, unpredictability, and
evasiveness in fully complying with United Nations (UN) resolutions. The Iraqi leader's actions were endangering his
country's territorial integrity, precluding its international rehabilitation, and postponing the removal of sanctions, thus
threatening in turn Jordan's own strategic and economic interests. In October 1994, when Iraq renewed tension by
concentrating forces near the Kuwaiti border, King Hussein
was unhesitating in his condemnation of the Iraqi action,
which, he said, was "totally irresponsible."[41] The king's complete disillusionment with Saddam eventually produced a
Jordanian experiment with interventionism, designed to has-
ten the downfall of the Iraqi ruler. In August 1995, Hussein
accorded safe haven to Saddam's two defecting sons-in-law,
Hussein Kamil and Saddam Kamil. He then suggested publicly that the time had come for change in Iraq, and that any
change would be "a change for the better."[42] In a speech to
the nation on August 23, Hussein recounted Saddam's record
of political folly, which he said had surprised and shocked
Jordan, from the Iran–Iraq war to the invasion of Kuwait. All
Jordan's offers of advice, he said, had "gone with the wind" to
the detriment of Jordan's state interests, which Iraq had consistently ignored.[43]

Yet the defiant Saddam was still popular with the Jordanian public, which overwhelmingly supported a hands-off
policy toward Iraq. These sentiments were aired in the press
as well as by members of parliament and the business community. Reflecting the public's disillusionment with this
apparent about-face toward Iraq following the defections, the
official position toward Iraq—especially that of the government, less so of Hussein himself—was therefore most
apologetic. In all probability, Hussein did seek to actively has-
ten the downfall of Saddam. Yet any policy to achieve this

end was only vaguely construed. Jordanian and Western diplomatic sources in Amman indicated that Jordan now sought
coordination with the United States, Saudi Arabia, and Kuwait to overthrow Saddam. At the same time, however, the
Jordanian government was constantly at pains to clarify that
Jordan remained committed to Iraqi integrity and sovereignty
and had no intention of interfering in its domestic affairs.
Moreover, the government insisted, Jordan had no intention
of severing its remaining economic ties with Iraq. U.S. efforts
at persuading the kingdom to tighten the sanctions on Iraq
failed against the Jordanian argument that no readily available alternative for low-cost Iraqi oil supplies existed, nor did
a substitute outlet for Jordanian exports.[44]

Exposed to conflicting external and domestic pressures,
Jordan's precise intentions and policy objectives remained
difficult to decipher. Seeking to facilitate change in Iraq without appearing to be meddling in Iraq's domestic affairs
required an almost impossible combination of verbal gym-
nastics and political acrobatics. King Hussein even gave rise
to speculation that he had his own personal ambitions in Iraq.
In his speech to the nation after the August 1995 defections,
as well as in other public statements at the time, he made
explicit references to the outstanding role of the Hashemites
in the history of Iraq, both in the early days of Islam and in
the modern era. It was, after all, a Hashemite monarchy that
ruled modern Iraq from its foundation in the 1920s until the
coup by 'Abd al-Karim Qasim in 1958. Hussein reminded his
people that he was heir to the Hashemite throne born of the
Jordanian–Iraqi union extant when his cousin, King Faysal
II, was overthrown. At the same time, however, he flatly denied that he himself entertained any ambition of becoming
king of Iraq, the mere thought of which, he said, would cause
"more trouble than it solved." If the Iraqi people wished to
install another Hashemite monarch, the decision would have
to be theirs.[45]

Rather than reflecting a desire to seek control of a post-
Saddam Iraq, King Hussein's statements on the Hashemites'

historical association with that country seemed intended to justify Jordan's new interventionist posture. The restoration of the Hashemite monarchy in Iraq indeed seemed farfetched. But Hussein's own ideas about Iraq at this stage were nevertheless usually predicated, by implication, on Saddam's ouster, and were based on three main points: (1) that Iraq come clean and fully implement all pertinent UN resolutions, as nothing short of compliance would lead to a lifting of the sanctions; (2) that it undergo "reform from within" toward the creation a pluralistic, democratic society; and (3) that the new system be founded on national reconciliation and federation among Iraq's three main sociopolitical components—Sunnis, Shi'is, and Kurds. Such a formula was imperative, the king maintained, to prevent the dismemberment of Iraq and to deny undue political gain to other potentially threatening forces in the region, an obvious reference to Iran.[46]

Meanwhile, if Hussein Kamil had been initially perceived by the Jordanians as the potential spearhead for change in Iraq, it did not take long for them to conclude that he was not the man for the job and that no political advantage would accrue from his presence in Amman. He had become more of a liability than an asset, and therefore the Jordanian leadership was relieved when the Kamil brothers returned to Iraq in late February 1996—although they were genuinely outraged by the family's summary execution in Baghdad. King Hussein was "disgusted" by the outcome and promised that Jordan would do all it could to "save Iraq" from its "ruthless leadership."[47]

Throughout this period, the king, along with Jordanian officials, pursued contacts and held meetings in London with representatives of the Iraqi opposition-in-exile. These were followed by numerous reports at the end of 1995 of a possible conference of Iraqi opposition movements to be held in Amman. The conference never took place because the inconsistencies of the kingdom's Iraq policy became more evident, but Jordan nevertheless continued to maintain contact with, and even host, representatives of the Iraqi opposition. The government also permitted the opening of three opposition party offices—although similar facilities were denied to many more such opposition groups.

Hussein had become a harsh critic of Saddam and would hardly have mourned his demise. But in practice, his country was incapable of doing very much to engineer such an outcome. Jordan's own inherent limitations, domestic opposition, and doubts about the length to which the United States was prepared to commit itself militarily to Saddam's ouster, along with the ineffectiveness of the Iraqi opposition-in-exile, all combined to induce the king, within but a few months, to lower his interventionist profile. Jordan soon reverted to its former more restrained policy of urging or pressuring Saddam to comply with the wishes of the international community in order to pave the way for Iraq's political and economic rehabilitation and the removal of debilitating sanctions.

Jordan continued to call for constitutional and democratic reform in Iraq but dropped the idea of federation, widely condemned in the Arab world as a partition proposal—which it was not. Although the Jordanians now wished to develop a coordinated Arab policy effecting change in Iraq, this, they explained, did not mean that Jordan was plotting to overthrow the Iraqi regime. Again, such a change would have to be made by the Iraqis themselves.

But there could be no mistaking a major transformation in Jordan's relations with Baghdad, and in early 1996, Jordan slashed its $400 million trade with Iraq by half because of the latter's heavily accumulated debt with the kingdom (some $1.2 billion) and its incapacity to pay for Jordanian imported goods.[48] Although this decision was motivated by economic rather than political calculations, King Hussein shortly thereafter appointed a new prime minister, 'Abd al-Karim Kabariti who as foreign minister had acquired a staunch anti-Iraqi reputation. By now, there was precious little left of the former alliance.

In the past, a similar deterioration in relations with Iraq would invariably have produced Jordanian overtures toward Syria. Such a shift, however, was not possible in post–Gulf War reality. The war had not caused any serious rupture in Jordan–Syria relations, but mutual trust between Syrian president Hafiz al-Asad and King Hussein remained far from certain with regard to Arab–Israeli issues. With the resumption of the peace process that had been set in motion by the Madrid Conference in October 1991, old mutual suspicions were revived as well. The Syrians were again particularly concerned about Jordan forging ahead into a separate deal with Israel. Indeed, as the Israeli–Jordanian negotiations gathered momentum after Madrid, Syrian censure of Jordan increased accordingly.[49]

King Hussein, however, was determined to proceed independently of the Syrian track, explaining that Jordan's own state interests (*al-khususiyya al-qutriyya*) compelled the kingdom to look after itself. These interests, particularly in the Palestinian arena, could not be subordinated to Syria's timetable or aspirations for regional domination. Indeed, Syria in the post–Cold War era, without the umbrella of the Soviet Union, was no longer capable of constraining either Jordan or the Palestinians from entering what was essentially a *pax Americana*. Asad denounced the Jordanian–Israeli peace treaty of 1994 while Hussein was confident enough to respond that, "with all due respect," Jordan's affairs were "none of [Asad's] business."[50] Matters were not made any easier by Syria's return to vintage pressure tactics like terrorism and political subversion, nor by its overexploitation of the waters of the Yarmuk River at Jordan's expense, which had serious implications for Jordan's already severe water shortage.[51] Simultaneously, Jordan's renewed security cooperation with the United States, its activism in Iraqi affairs, and its enhanced ties with Turkey only aggravated relations further, as the Syrians perceived Jordan to be collaborating with the United States and its regional allies to drive Syria into isolation. In sum, for much of the 1990s, the Jordanian–Syrian relationship was frigid, hardly a basis for an alternative alliance.[52]

Weathering the Storm between Jordan and Its Traditional Allies

Jordan found greater success in repairing relations with its traditional allies, although with Saudi Arabia—much less Kuwait—this was a far more protracted and agonizing process than with the United States. Indeed, the sense of betrayal felt by Saudis and Kuwaitis was difficult to overcome. The Saudis initially rebuffed Jordanian approaches, but the Kuwaitis made it quite clear that they would not just "let bygones be bygones." Relations with Jordan were of far greater importance to the neighboring Saudis than to the distant Kuwaitis. The Saudis, according to a Western diplomat, were "at least willing to listen," but for the Kuwaitis "it [was] personal." They had "written off the king."[53]

Even so, only in late 1995, when Jordan's rupture with Saddam had become more obvious, did relations with Saudi Arabia begin to show signs of repair. A Saudi ambassador returned to Amman in November after an absence of five years, and in August 1996, Hussein met with King Fahd for the first time since 1990. The Jordanians believed that this landmark event had "sealed Jordanian–Saudi reconciliation,"[54] even though they did not entertain high expectations for renewed aid from the oil-producing Arab states, which were not as wealthy as they were in the heyday of the oil boom. Indeed, Saudi aid to Jordan was not renewed, but the Saudis did reopen their market to Jordanian labor, a crucial move for the Jordanian economy.[55]

Relations with Saudi Arabia continued to improve thereafter. Particularly encouraging from the Jordanian point of view was the fact that these relations had been reestablished on an even keel of stability, cordiality, and regular high-level contact between Hussein and Hassan and their Saudi counterparts, King Fahd and Crown Prince 'Abdullah.[56] The Saudis even tried their hand at mediating between Syria and Jordan, although they did not meet with success.

Saudi Arabia continued to remain tightfisted, however, when it came to economic aid. In mid-1997, it was reported that the Saudis had committed themselves to assist Jordan if it faced economic crisis, but that the aid would be conditional upon Jordan's distancing itself from Israel.[57] During 1998, when the Jordanians feared that U.S. air strikes against Iraq might lead to an interruption of their oil supply, the Saudis promised to supply Jordan with oil—but at market price, rather than at the preferential rate Jordan had obtained from Iraq.[58] In any event, the need for such a supply did not arise.

Saudi concerns for Jordanian stability were heightened by the transition from Hussein to 'Abdallah II in February 1999. The Saudis were swift to announce their readiness to "use [their] resources to support Jordan."[59] Jordan's role as a buffer between Saudi Arabia and Syria was, after all, more important to the Saudi monarchy than the after-effects of Gulf War hostility and suspicion. Although the Saudis reiterated that relations between the two monarchies were "stronger than words,"[60] Saudi pledges of support were not easily translated into deeds.

Generally speaking, the bottom line seemed to be that the Saudis would do what it took to prevent the collapse of the Jordanian economy by providing an "insurance policy" of last resort, but they would not go out of their way to be generous. Whether this position stemmed from a residue of Gulf War hostility or from Saudi economic constraints was not entirely clear.[61] Whatever the explanation, it made little difference to the Jordanians, who could no longer rely on Saudi Arabia for regular infusions of economic aid as they had done in the 1970s and 1980s during the greatest era of Saudi oil wealth. The Jordanians themselves claimed that they were "not looking for a single shot-in-the-arm cash payment" but rather for a further reopening of the Saudi market to Jordanian labor and the resumption of Jordanian agricultural exports to Saudi Arabia.[62] These measures, however, could not be taken for granted. Before resuming agricultural imports from Jordan, the Saudis sought assurances that the crops for import were being irrigated with fresh, clean water and not purified waste water. This was a demand that most Jordanian farmers could not meet, and as a result, although trade with Iraq had declined considerably in the previous few years, Saudi Arabia still trailed behind Iraq in second place on the list of Jordan's main Arab trading partners.[63]

As for the Kuwaitis, they too mellowed with time. Slight improvements in ties with Jordan were apparent in early 1997 when Kuwait began to release some of the few dozen Jordanian prisoners held for collaborating with the Iraqis during the Gulf War. Trade relations were resumed in March 1997 and commercial flights between Jordan and Kuwait were renewed in July.[64] In May 1998, Kuwait released another group of Jordanian prisoners, a move followed by further indications of a more substantive thaw as Jordan's relations with Iraq continued to founder. An exchange of high-level visits took place in January 1999, and in late February, the last Jordanians still held in Kuwait were set free. Finally, in March 1999, the Jordanian embassy in Kuwait was officially reopened, setting the stage for what appeared to be complete reconciliation between the two countries.

Notes

1. Asher Susser, "Jordan," *Middle East Contemporary Survey (MECS)*, vol. I (1976–77), p. 586; vol. II (1977–78), p. 591.

2. Susser, "Jordan," *MECS*, vol. IV (1979–80), pp. 582–583; Amatzia Baram, "Baathi Iraq and Hashimite Jordan: From Hostility to Alignment," *Middle East Journal* 45, no. 1 (Winter 1991), pp. 55–56; Joseph Nevo, "Jordan's Relations with Iraq: Ally or Victim?" in Amatzia Baram and Barry Rubin, eds., *Iraq's Road to War* (New York: St. Martin's Press, 1994), p. 139.

3. Laurie Brand, *Jordan's Inter-Arab Relations: The Political Economy of Alliance Making* (New York: Columbia University Press, 1994), pp. 94–95.

4. Hussein as quoted in *Al-Ra'y*, January 12, 1981.

5. Radio Amman April 9, in Federal Broadcasting Information Service *Daily Report–Near East and South Asia* (FBIS), April 10, 1980.

6. Radio Amman, June 8, in FBIS, June 9, 1981; Susser, "Jordan," *MECS*, vol. IV (1979–80), pp. 582–584; vol. V (1980–81), p. 649.

7. Baram, "Baathi Iraq," pp. 63–65.

8. Syrian official source, as quoted in Radio Damascus, February 21, in

SWB (*Summary of World Broadcasting*, British Broadcasting Corp.) February 23, 1981.

9. Baram, "Baathi Iraq," p. 65; Susser, "Jordan," *MECS*, vol. IV (1979–80), p. 583; vol. V (1980–81), p. 651; vol. VI (1981–82), p. 690; vol. VIII (1983–84), p. 526; vol. IX (1984–85), p. 520; Jordan TV, November 10, in FBIS, November 12, 1985.

10. Brand, *Jordan's Inter-Arab Relations*, p. 196.

11. Ibid., p. 215.

12. Susser, "Jordan," *MECS*, vol. XII (1988), p. 606-607; vol. XIII (1989), p. 471; vol. XIV (1990), pp. 482, 490.

13. Susser, "Jordan," *MECS*, vol. XII (1988), p. 607; vol. XIII (1989), pp. 452–454; Nevo, "Jordan's Relations with Iraq," pp. 143–144; Baram, "Baathi Iraq," pp. 57–58; Brand, p. 230.

14. Amatzia Baram, "No New Fertile Crescent: Iraqi-Jordanian Relations, 1968–92," in Joseph Nevo and Ilan Pappe, eds., *Jordan in the Middle East, 1948–1988: The Making of a Pivotal State* (London: Frank Cass, 1994), p. 136.

15. Radio Amman, December 8, in FBIS, December 9, 1988; Susser, "Jordan," *MECS*, vol. XII (1988), p. 606.

16. *Jordan Times*, January 20, 1990; Susser, "Jordan," *MECS*, vol. XIV (1990), p. 482.

17. *Sawt al-Sha'b* (Amman), April 19, 1990; Susser, "Jordan," *MECS*, vol. XIV (1990), p. 483.

18. Hassan Bin Talal, *Search for Peace: The Politics of the Middle Ground in the Arab East* (New York: St. Martin's Press, 1984), p. 99.

19. Susser, "Jordan," *MECS*, vol. XIV (1990), pp. 483–484, 491.

20. *Jordan Times*, December 1, 9, 30; Jordan TV December 25, in FBIS, December 26, 1990; Susser, "Jordan," *MECS*, vol. XIV (1990), pp. 484–485.

21. *Jordan Times*, October 9, 1990; Susser, "Jordan," *MECS*, vol. XIV (1990), pp. 485–486.

22. Susser, "Jordan," *MECS*, vol. XIV (1990), pp. 485–486.

23. *Jordan Times*, December 19, 1990.

24. Susser, "Jordan," *MECS*, vol. XIV (1990), pp. 488–489.

25. Baram, "Baathi Iraq," p. 69.

26. Susser, "Jordan," *MECS*, vol. XIV (1990), p. 491.

27. The author would like to thank Adiba Mango for clarifying these points to him.

28. Susser, "Jordan," *MECS*, vol. XII (1988), p. 608.

29. Brand, *Jordan's Inter-Arab Relations*, p. 122.

30. Susser, "Jordan," *MECS*, vol. XIV (1990), p. 492.

31. *Jordan Times*, October 28, 1990; Susser, "Jordan," *MECS*, vol. XIV (1990), p. 493.

32. All quotes from Radio Amman, February 6, in FBIS, February 7, 1991; Susser, "Jordan," *MECS*, vol. XV (1991), pp. 502–503.

33. *Jordan Times*, April 14, 1991; Susser, "Jordan," *MECS*, vol. XV (1991), pp. 486–487.

34. *Jordan Times*, May 27, 1995.

35. *Jordan Times*, May 23, 1995.

36. Susser, "Jordan," *MECS*, vol. XV (1991), pp. 487–488; vol. XIX (1995), p. 422.

37. *Jordan Times*, January 29, 1991.

38. *Al-Ra'y*, December 12, 1991.

39. Susser, "Jordan," *MECS*, vol. XV (1991), pp. 487–488; vol. XX (1996), pp. 423–424.

40. Susser, "Jordan," *MECS*, vol. XV (1991), pp. 503–504.

41. Jordan TV, October 11, in FBIS, October 12, 1994; Susser, "Jordan," *MECS*, vol. XVI (1992), pp. 558–559; vol. XVII (1993), p. 477; vol. XVIII (1994), p. 430.

42. *Yediot Aharonot*, August, 14, 1995.

43. Jordan TV, August 23, in FBIS, August 24, 1995; Susser, "Jordan," *MECS*, vol. XIX (1995), pp. 415–416.

44. Susser, "Jordan," *MECS*, vol. XIX (1995), p. 416.

45. Susser, "Jordan," *MECS*, vol. XIX (1995), pp. 417–418.

46. *Al-Quds al-Arabi*, August 21, 1995; Susser, "Jordan," *MECS*, vol. XIX (1995), p. 418.

47. *Al-Dustur*, February 13, 1996; Susser, "Jordan," *MECS*, vol. XX (1996), p. 445.

48. *Al-Hayat*, January 24, 1996; Susser, "Jordan," *MECS*, vol. XIX (1995), pp. 414–419; vol. XX (1996), p. 446.

49. Susser, "Jordan," *MECS*, vol. XVI (1992), pp. 560–561; vol. XVII (1993), pp. 478–479; vol. XVIII (1994), pp. 428–429.

50. Jordan TV, October 25, in FBIS, October 26, 1994.

51. Arnon Sofer, "Jordan Facing the 1990s: Location, Metropolis, and Water," in Nevo and Pappe, eds., *Jordan in the Middle East, 1948–1988*, pp. 39–41.

52. Susser, "Jordan," *MECS*, vol. XVIII (1994), pp. 428–429; vol. XIX (1995), p. 420; vol. XX (1996), pp. 446–447.

53. *New York Times*, November 25, 1993.

54. *Al-Hayat*, August 13, 1996.

55. Susser, "Jordan," *MECS*, vol. XV (1991), p. 511; vol. XVI (1992), p. 560; vol. XVII (1993), p. 479; vol. XVIII (1994), pp. 418, 429; vol. XIX (1995), p. 420; vol. XX (1996), p. 447.

56. *Jordan Times*, January 25; September 18–19, 1997.

57. *Jordan Times*, June 5–6; *al-Urdunn*, June 7; *al-Hadath* (FBIS online), June 23 1997 (date listed for FBIS online citations is original date of publication).

58. *Al-Dustur*, February 8; Agence France Presse (FBIS online), December 17, 1998.

59. *Jordan Times*, February 9, 1999.

60. Ibid.

61. For more on lingering Gulf War hostility, see *Al-Urdunn*, May 9, 1998.

62. *Jordan Times*, February 20, 1999.

63. *Jordan Times*, March 2, July 4, August 11, 1999.

64. *Jordan Times*, February 25; *al-Watan*, March 5 (FBIS online); *Jordan Times*, July 10–11, 1997.

Chapter 5

Jordan between Israel and
the Arab Hinterland

Geographic proximity and demographic reality make it virtually impossible for Jordan to escape the potential impact of any conflict—or settlement—related to the Palestinian question. Situated on the "doorstep of Palestine," Jordan has always been deeply involved and profoundly affected by the Arab–Israeli struggle over the fate of that land, and particularly by the conflict's demographic impact. The conquest by Jordan of the West Bank in 1948 resulted in a transformation of the kingdom into a country with a large Palestinian majority (about half of whom were refugees from what had become Israel). The constant migration of Palestinians from the West Bank to the East Bank during Jordanian rule continued during much of the Israeli occupation that began with the 1967 war. Furthermore, some 250,000–300,000 Palestinian refugees fled from the West Bank to the East Bank in the wake of this conflict, and a similar number of Palestinians left Kuwait for Jordan during the Gulf War. By most accounts, the Palestinians by the early 1990s had become a majority on the East Bank, with a population more or less equal to the Palestinian population in the West Bank and Gaza combined (more than 2 million).

Sandwiched between Israel on the one hand and Iraq on the other, Jordan has sought to protect its interests in the Palestinian question through strategic vacillation between these two mighty neighbors. When at war with Israel, for example, Jordan has obtained Iraqi military assistance (as in 1948 and 1967). But more often than not, Jordan has tried to protect itself and its Palestinian interests through some kind

69

of tacit understanding, or *modus vivendi,* with Israel. Jordan's alliance with Iraq in the 1980s was intimately connected to the kingdom's perception of a new Israeli threat. Then, true to historical pattern, relations with Iraq declined in the early 1990s as Jordan advanced toward peace with Israel. As relations with Israel improved, Jordan could consequently afford to distance itself further from Iraq.

Perceptions of the Israeli Threat

After decades of common understanding based on mutual interest with successive Labor governments in Israel, the rise to power of the right-wing Likud party in 1977, and particularly its reelection in 1981, had an unsettling effect on the Jordan–Israel relationship. In the Jordanian view, the return to office of Menahem Begin was ample indication that a sizable majority of Israelis approved of his policies—a notion that King Hussein found ominous for the future. Jordanian leaders in the early 1980s often expressed their assessment that Israel enjoyed unchallenged military superiority, and under the Likud it had no intention of withdrawing from the West Bank and Gaza. Amman also feared that Israel might seek to solve its own demographic problems by expelling large numbers of Palestinians from the occupied territories to Jordan as a forerunner to, or consequence of, Israeli annexation of those territories.[1]

From the time of the kingdom's violent struggle with the Palestinians in the late 1960s and early 1970s, Jordanians expressed the fear that some in the Arab world or in Israel actually sought the establishment of an "alternative homeland" for the Palestinians in Jordan. Statements such as those made at the time by Tunisia's Habib Bourguiba, mentioned previously, suggested that these suspicions were not entirely groundless, and Jordanian nerves became so frayed by the possibility that even the United States was not above suspicion. When newly elected President Jimmy Carter spoke in early 1977 in favor of a Palestinian homeland possibly to be connected with Jordan, Jordanians immediately became concerned that Carter might have embraced the idea of a Palestinian state in the East Bank. It took some effort on the part of the Americans to reassure King Hussein that this was not, in fact, what they had in mind.[2]

Jordanian anxieties were also easily exacerbated by the idea promoted by some in Israel's Likud government that Jordan was in fact a Palestinian state (the "Jordan is Palestine" option), and that the solution to the Palestinian problem ought to be found in the formal transformation of Jordan into Palestine. This notion came to be known in Jordanian domestic political parlance as the "alternative homeland conspiracy" (*mu'amarat al-watan al-badil*).[3] When Israel invaded Lebanon in 1982 and Defense Minister Ariel Sharon made reference to the creation of a new Middle East map, Jordanian concerns were heightened even further. Hussein concluded that it was not only Lebanon that Israel had in mind, but probably Jordan as well. He even expressed the fear that Israel might trigger another war in which his kingdom could be "the next target," facilitating the establishment of an "alternative homeland" for the Palestinians there.[4]

Such an act of mass expulsion by Israel was hardly a realistic option. Jordanian fears, however, were genuine. Throughout the 1980s, the Jordanians seemed obsessed with what Prince Hassan described as potential Israeli "demographic aggression."[5] King Hussein's analysis follows: Israel would rapidly approach a serious dilemma if it chose not to withdraw from the West Bank and Gaza. It would either have to forfeit its Jewish character by granting citizenship to the Palestinians in the occupied territories, or abandon its democratic nature and be forced to adopt the apartheid model of South Africa. The Israelis, he feared, might seek to resolve this dilemma through a mass eviction of Palestinians to Jordan. This last option, Hussein seemed to believe at the time, was gaining support in Israel and "coloring the current Israeli political vision with an extremist right-wing hue."[6]

At the end of the decade, against the background of an expected mass Jewish emigration to Israel from the Soviet

Union, Hussein and Hassan publicly charged that Israel was indeed posing the "threat of transfer." Israel, they said, sought to "drive [the Palestinians] across the river into Jordan and other Arab countries in a bid to make way for newcomers."[7] This was reported at the time to be the king's "worst nightmare," and concern by Jordanian officials was reputedly "bordering on panic."[8] Hussein subsequently regarded the formation of a new, entirely right-wing government in Israel (replacing the national unity, Labor–Likud government dissolved in March 1990) as a patent threat, and he further expected "attempts [to] continue to uproot [the Palestinians] or force them to abandon their land. Officials in Israel might also think it is opportune to change the status quo, not just in the occupied territories but also in the neighborhood, in order to guarantee [Israel's] security and safety for a very long time to come."[9]

Hussein concluded that time was not on the Arabs' side, which prompted two different, but complementary, responses. One response was to appeal for an urgent resumption of the Arab–Israeli peace process before Jordan was "swept away by a tide of radicalism" that could overtake the region in the absence of progress;[10] the other was to seek strategic protection once again by cementing an alliance with Iraq.

Jordan, Israel, and the Gulf War

By the time of the Gulf War (1990–91), prevailing circumstances hardly seemed conducive to a strategic understanding between Jordan and Israel. Jordan had by then established particularly close ties with Iraq, which included elements of military cooperation that Israel found particularly disconcerting. But while Hussein sought Iraqi protection against Israel, he was at the same time cautious not to provoke the Israelis.[11] From the onset of the crisis, Israel expressed its concern about the possible deployment of Iraqi forces in Jordan, warning that such a development would not be tolerated and that Israel would use force to prevent it. The Jordanians declared that their kingdom would "not [be] a passage for anybody, one way or the other," and that they would protect its sovereignty "against all comers."[12] If there were no Israeli intentions to attack Jordan, then there would be no need for any outside forces to be stationed there.[13] Israel repeatedly assured the Jordanians, both in public statements by Prime Minister Yitzhak Shamir and Chief of Staff Lt. Gen. Dan Shomron and through third parties, that it had no intention of undermining Jordanian stability. Yet, despite these Israeli assurances, the Jordanians remained apprehensive that Israel might exploit the crisis as a pretext to impose the Jordan is Palestine solution forcefully.[14]

When faced with the immediate threat of a major conflagration in the region, Jordan and Israel—right-wing government notwithstanding—were still capable of establishing a *modus vivendi* to secure Jordanian stability and territorial integrity. In January 1991, on the eve of Operation Desert Storm, Hussein and Shamir met secretly in London. Hussein was extremely concerned that Jordan might be dragged into a regional conflict in which it had no desire to be involved. Keenly aware of the kingdom's vulnerability and its "geopolitically thankless position," his objectives were to ensure that Jordan would be spared the ravages of war, that his kingdom would not become "the killing ground" in a potential confrontation between Israel and Iraq, and that Israel would not exploit the situation to force Palestinians out of the West Bank into Jordan.

Hussein assured Shamir that Jordan was no longer engaged in military cooperation with Iraq, that it would not permit the deployment of Iraqi forces in Jordan, and that it would prevent Iraqi aircraft from flying through Jordanian airspace. In return, the king sought an Israeli commitment to refrain from any infringement upon Jordan's territorial integrity—by land or air—in the conduct of military operations against Iraq. (Hussein's request from Israel was based on the hope that he would be able to extract a similar commitment from Saddam Husayn.) Shamir acceded to King Hussein's request, but added that Israel reserved the right to respond as it deemed necessary in the event of an Iraqi advance into Jordan.[15]

When it came to war, Israel laid no blame on the Jordanians for the Iraqi Scud missile attacks on Israeli cities, even though the missiles passed through Jordanian air space; it was obvious that Jordan could not have prevented the attacks. In fact, one of the reasons for Israel's decision to refrain from retaliation (aside from considerations related to sensitivities of the Arab partners in the American coalition against Iraq) lay in Shamir's determination to honor his commitment to Hussein and not draw Jordan into the fray.[16]

King Hussein was reported by an Israeli source to have been encouraged by Israel's restraint and its refusal to exploit the situation for the sake of implementing the Jordan is Palestine option that Jordan feared so profoundly.[17] Moreover, months after the war had ended, Shamir made a point of impressing upon Secretary of State James Baker the need for more generous U.S. aid to Jordan and for continued support of the kingdom's stability for the sake of long-term peace in the region.[18]

The Peace Imperative

Despite Shamir's request from Washington, Jordan was strategically and economically beleaguered in the aftermath of the Gulf War. Its strategic and economic Iraqi hinterland had been crushed, and, after having refused to join the allied coalition against Iraq, the kingdom's relations with its traditional allies in the United States and the Gulf had been seriously ruptured. Of Jordan's two policy options for dealing with the challenge of Israel—forging an alliance with Iraq or pursuing the Arab–Israeli peace process—only the second alternative had any validity in the postwar reality.

With the onset of the Madrid Conference in 1991, Jordan desperately needed to work its way back into the good graces of the United States, for the sake of both strategic protection and economic security. When Secretary Baker met with Hussein in Aqaba for the first time after the war in April 1991, they quickly agreed to "let bygones be bygones,"[19] as long as the Jordanians enlisted actively in the American-sponsored peace process at Madrid. Congress was far less tolerant toward Hussein's Gulf War behavior, but it was strongly opposed by the Bush administration when it sought to cut aid to Jordan. Spokesmen for the administration explained that the kingdom was "critical politically [and] geographically" and that its stability was important to Israel, to the region as a whole, and to the advancement of the peace process.[20] Although Congress nevertheless remained displeased with Jordan, particularly as the kingdom violated United Nations (UN) sanctions against Iraq, the administration had clearly chosen to "turn a blind eye" to Jordanian behavior.[21]

In addition to strategic protection, defense cooperation with the United States, and a reduced threat of conflict with Israel, Jordan also coveted enhanced opportunities for trade, investment, and economic development. Averting disaster with emergency economic aid was one thing; securing stable, sustainable progress and prosperity was quite another. Under these circumstances, peace with Israel had become an urgent imperative. Jawad al-'Anani, a former Jordanian cabinet minister and leading economic analyst, acknowledged that the kingdom's entire future depended on the Middle East peace process.[22]

Shortly before the signing of Jordan's 1994 treaty with Israel, King Hussein elaborated on his strategic rationale for peace. In the aftermath of the Gulf War, he explained, Jordan was in a grave predicament. The kingdom lacked stability and also suffered from severe economic difficulties. It was threatened from every side at a time when it enjoyed neither superpower protection nor that of any international alliance or organization. Even in the Arab arena, Jordan was still experiencing the consequences of its own actions during the Gulf crisis and had no truly reliable allies. If the kingdom were endangered, the king warned, there would be "nobody to back it."[23] The future of Jordan, he seemed to say, was hanging in the balance. Jordan was urgently in need of American support, particularly for debt relief and the modernization of its armed forces. This kind of aid, however, would not be forthcoming without congressional support, which was particularly difficult to achieve after the Gulf War (as illustrated above) and clearly dependent on Jordan's participation in the peace process.[24]

What was King Hussein to do, asked a Jordanian analyst, if his country, cash-strapped and militarily weak, refused to "play ball" with the Americans and the Israelis? "Turning to Europe and Japan was hardly an option. These took their cue from Washington anyway . . . all of which left the king no option but to compromise long-held principles if his country was not to disintegrate."[25] Jordan's problems, according to another Jordanian observer, had generated "a frantic willingness to do whatever [was] required of it to survive."[26]

In the Jordanian analysis, the regional balance of power had, on the whole, shifted in Israel's favor as a result of Iraq's defeat in the Gulf War, the loss of the Arab oil weapon, and the disintegration of the Soviet Union. As the United States was now the "only country that decides matters," and as America was committed to dealing effectively with the Arab–Israeli conflict, Hussein argued, there could be "no room for procrastination."[27] A window of opportunity was open, and no alternative to peaceful settlement existed "except disaster."[28] Indeed, the initiation of the Madrid peace process in October 1991 set Israel–Jordan relations on a new course of formal reconciliation, as Jordan now sought reassurance from Israel rather than the deterrence value of Iraqi "strategic depth."

The accession to power of the more flexible Labor Party in June 1992 added impetus and confidence to the Madrid process, eroded only briefly by the surprise of the Oslo accords signed between Israel and the Palestine Liberation Organization (PLO) in September 1993. Jordan and Israel had already reached an essentially agreed-upon agenda in October 1992, but the Jordanians, unwilling to face accusations of outpacing the Palestinians, repeatedly clarified that they would not formally ratify the agenda until similar progress was made on the other tracks—specifically that of the Israelis and Palestinians. Jordan, they said, would not enter into a separate peace treaty with Israel. Although agreements could be reached in the bilateral negotiating tracks of the Madrid process, they would have to be implemented within the context of a comprehensive settlement. For "the final ratification of peace," said Hussein, all parties had "to come together," or, as Premier 'Abd al-Salam al-Majali noted, all had to "move forward in tandem."[29]

The Impact of the Oslo Surprise

But the Oslo accords changed this posture. Before, Jordan had genuinely supported "independent Palestinian decision making" and direct PLO involvement in the peace process, but an agreement reached in secret between Israel and the PLO to the total exclusion of Jordan was considerably more than the Jordanians were prepared to handle. They were shocked, if not stunned, by the Oslo accords, which seemed designed—at least by the PLO—to cut the Jordanians out of any influential role regarding the future of the West Bank and to challenge Jordanian interests over such items as Jerusalem, refugees, and the ultimate demarcation of borders.

Jordanians have since complained that their Israeli interlocutors did not always understand the nuances of the Jordanian position in their communications and contact because of Hussein's style of negotiation and conversational manner. The Jordanians often did not spell out particularly sensitive matters, and much was left to the intuition of their Israeli counterparts; consequently, subtle messages were not always interpreted correctly. For instance, Jordanian silence in a conversation instead of explicit refutation was sometimes understood by the Israelis to mean acceptance, when in fact it did not.[30]

The complexity of the Jordanian position on Palestinian representation and the precise measure of involvement desired by the Jordanian negotiators seem to have been casualties of this somewhat ambiguous mode of communication. Jordan favored PLO participation in the peace process and genuinely believed that it was in the kingdom's own self-interest for the Palestinians to bear full responsibility for any settlement of the Palestinian question. The Jordanians had received more than enough condemnation in the past from their Arab brethren for their efforts in and involvement with the issue, and consequently were not interested in negotiating for the Palestinians in the present circumstances. But this did not mean that they expected to be ignored and marginalized, particularly on matters so crucial to their own vital interests. On the contrary, the Jordanians sought, and continue to seek, coordination, consultation, and, wherever possible, strategic understanding with both Israel and the Palestinians. Indeed, the entire Palestinian solution affects Jordan more directly than it affects any other regional player, aside from the two protagonists themselves.

Since Oslo, the Jordanians have developed a more forthright manner, presenting their positions more explicitly to their Israeli interlocutors (with an unusual bluntness when former Prime Minister Binyamin Netanyahu was in office), thereby clarifying their interests, concerns, and consequent expectations for a say in final status negotiations with the Palestinians.

But in the immediate aftermath of the Oslo accords, the Jordanians concluded that their earlier policy of waiting for progress on other tracks had not born fruit, having instead produced some of the most undesirable consequences. The time had come for Jordan to abandon "its docile image." It could not wait passively for the "future [to] unfold itself."[31] The fate of the kingdom was at stake, and as Prince Hassan observed, it was time for Jordan to put itself first. As he told the London *Observer*, "The world is going to turn around and say 'bugger you' unless you get your act together."[32] On September 14, the day after the PLO and Israel had formally signed the Oslo accords at the White House (September 13), Jordan and Israel signed their agreed-upon agenda, which had been left in abeyance since October 1992.

Above all else, the Jordanians were most immediately concerned about the possible impact of the emerging Palestinian entity on the sensitive and potentially volatile relationship between Jordanians and Palestinians on the East Bank. Hussein was particularly disturbed by surfacing tensions between citizens of Palestinian origin and their East Bank compatriots on the issue of ultimate Palestinian loyalties. An emerging trend among the East Banker elite suggested that the time had come for Palestinians in Jordan to consider exercising political rights in their embryonic homeland of Palestine rather than in Jordan. Accordingly, in the first few months after Oslo, Hussein spoke with unusual intensity in his public statements, warning that anyone tampering with national unity would be his "enemy until doomsday."[33] Palestinians in Jordan, the king noted, enjoyed all rights of citizenship and would continue to do so unhindered unless they themselves freely elected to leave for Palestine. The king's forceful stand stifled public debate but did not resolve the fundamental problem nor eliminate the accompanying sensitivities. As final status talks approach between Israelis and Palestinians on the current political scene, the subject is likely to be a major issue on Jordan's agenda.

Jordanians were similarly troubled by their assessment of the economic ramifications stemming from the Oslo agreement. Fearing permanent exclusion from the compatible and potentially lucrative Palestinian market, Jordan sought to convince the Palestinians that close ties with Jordan's economy instead of Israel's would be both politically and economically advantageous and would reduce the Palestinians' dependence on the much more powerful Israeli economy. But the Palestinians, always suspicious of Jordanian ulterior motives, remained unconvinced.

Jordan's other economic concerns related to the international community, specifically the possibility that much of the international aid to the region would now be channeled to the Palestinians—at Jordan's expense. Jordanians were therefore eager to make the point that the kingdom had to be taken into account in any allocation of aid, considering the hardships it had undergone during the long years of Middle

East conflict and the more recent Gulf crisis. Moreover, they would argue, the economic well-being of the newborn Palestinian entity could not be achieved in isolation from Jordan.

Strategic Anxieties and the Israeli–Jordanian Treaty

The Jordanians were obviously concerned that the Oslo accords were the harbinger of a Palestine-centric process whereby Jordan would gradually lose its geopolitical value to Israel and to other key players in the international community. Strategic interest in the kingdom's well-being had heretofore, at least in part, been a function of the moderating influence Jordan had exercised through its involvement in the Palestinian arena. But now the kingdom desperately needed a new platform of strategic understanding with Israel. For half a century, Israel's inability or unwillingness to come to terms with the Palestinian national movement had created a vested Israeli interest in a stable Jordan as an anchor to contain Palestinian militancy. The Jordanians were now apparently concerned that Israel's breakthrough with the PLO had driven that historical interest into the throes of reassessment.

Apparently at Hussein's request, the king and Prime Minister Yitzhak Rabin met secretly just a few weeks after the signing of the Oslo accords. At this meeting, the Jordanians vented their displeasure about the Oslo surprise while simultaneously seeking reassurances from Israel. Rabin reportedly did assure the king that Israel's traditional policy toward Jordan had not changed. Israel sought both the rapid incorporation of Jordan into the peace process and a strong link between Jordan and a future Palestinian entity.[34] Mutual trust between Israel and the PLO was, after all, far from complete.

Even so, the Jordanians were still not ready for a peace treaty with Israel so soon after Oslo. They remained uncertain as to whether that country's agreement with the Palestinians would, in fact, be implemented and were similarly wary of Syrian opposition to a Jordanian separate deal. In this regard, Jordan consistently reaffirmed that the kingdom was committed to a comprehensive peace between Israel and all of its Arab neighbors and that it would not sign a separate peace treaty with Israel. The novelty in Jordan's position at this juncture was that the kingdom's leadership apparently no longer believed it had to wait for progress on other tracks of the peace process before at least moving ahead substantively in talks with Israel, and that only the signing of treaties between Israel and her Arab neighbors should be done in tandem.

Three primary external factors prompted the Jordanians to move ahead into talks with Israel:

1. The Palestinians. Israel and the Palestinians signed an economic agreement at the end of April 1994 in Paris, and another agreement in early May of that year in Cairo, pertaining to the implementation of the Declaration of Principles in Gaza and Jericho. These agreements had the dual effect of both reassuring the Jordanians that Oslo was indeed being implemented and arousing anxieties that the kingdom was being excluded and marginalized on political and economic issues of major interest to Jordan in the West Bank. In any case, there was no real Jordanian–Palestinian coordination. The Palestinians were not exhibiting the slightest concern for Jordanian interests, choosing to inform Amman of their decisions and activities only after the fact. Furthermore, the Jordanians were exasperated by Palestinian procrastination in arriving at any form of strategic understanding with the kingdom. Hussein finally concluded that "enough was enough" and that the time had come for Jordan to take control of its own destiny.[35] In his own words, considering "its interlinkage with the Palestinian issue," the kingdom could not lag behind.[36] Or, as another leading Jordanian figure explained, Jordan was compelled to protect its own "strategic interests threatened by the ramifications of the Palestinian–Israeli agreement."[37] Moreover, Hussein was anxious to maintain at least a measure of influence with the embryonic Palestinian state emerging on his kingdom's border.[38]

2. *The Syrians.* Although it was argued that Jordan could not wait for progress on the Syrian track if it meant losing ground in the meantime on the all-important Palestinian issue, Jordanian spokesmen repeatedly contended that there was, in fact, progress on the Syrian front. In a closed meeting with members of the Jordanian Chamber of Deputies in early June 1994, Prime Minister Majali told his audience that there was already an agreement between the United States and Syria on the "basic contours" of an Israeli–Syrian settlement. But it was never quite clear whether pronouncements like this one reflected a genuine assessment or merely served as a justification for going ahead of the Syrians to forge a separate peace. In any event, with the demise of the Soviet Union, Syria had lost much of its regional influence, and it no longer held a veto over the Palestinians or the Jordanians. King Hussein also resented the Syrian tendency to dominate the Jordan–Syria relationship, making coordination on an equal footing unattainable. He and Hafiz al-Asad did reach an agreement to move ahead together on negotiations with Israel, but Asad could apparently afford to bide his time while Jordan could not;[39] nor was Hussein prepared to wait and enter negotiations with Israel in a much weaker bargaining position.[40]

3. *The United States and the Israeli–Jordanian Front.* As negotiations gained momentum, Israeli foreign minister Shimon Peres issued reassuring statements in mid-July clarifying that, for Israel, "Jordan is not Palestine . . . Jordan is Jordan and Palestine is Palestine."[41] Israel, he stressed, had no intention of altering the character of the Hashemite Kingdom. For the Jordanians, Peres's statements were a welcome reaffirmation of Israel's interest in the kingdom's stability. But the highlight of this new atmosphere of progress was the landmark meeting on July 25, 1994, in Washington between King Hussein and Prime Minister Rabin, in which the two leaders conferred in public for the first time. At this meeting, Hussein and Rabin issued

the Washington Declaration, in which they announced the termination of the state of belligerency between their two countries and reaffirmed the commitment to "vigorously continue" their negotiations in order to "arrive at a state of peace." Israel also declared its respect for the "present special role of the Hashemite Kingdom of Jordan in Muslim holy shrines in Jerusalem" and undertook to "give high priority to the Jordanian historic role in these shrines" in future permanent status negotiations.[42] This White House encounter was followed by a joint appearance of the two leaders before both houses of Congress the next day. Jordanian officials explained that the Washington meeting was intended to mobilize congressional support for a commitment by the U.S. administration to write off Jordan's debt and provide military aid. (The administration had urged the Jordanians to make a high-profile gesture of goodwill to Israel as a precondition for such congressional approval.) Indeed, the Jordanians expected a treaty with Israel to pave the way for such debt relief by the United States (and its allies), as well as for aid and equipment designated for the modernization of Jordan's armed forces.

From this point onward, it was clear that the conclusion of a full-fledged peace treaty between the two countries was only a matter of time and timing,[43] and indeed on October 26, 1994, just three months after the Washington Declaration, Jordan and Israel signed a treaty. Since neither party regarded direct military attack by the other as a major threat, the treaty makes no reference at all to bilateral security arrangements such as demilitarization, early warning stations, or foreign supervision—arrangements that are so central to the Israel–Egypt treaty and to the Israel–Syria negotiations. Instead, it relates to the perennial regional strategic anxieties held by both Jordan and Israel that were not only ever-present in the negotiations, but arguably constitute the main substance of the agreement. Jordan's preoccupation with the specter of Palestinian expulsion by Israel as a so-called "demographic

aggression" and Israel's fundamental interest in the preservation of Jordan as a stable buffer between Israel and Iraq
were both key issues crafted into the treaty in this regard. In
reference to Israel's concerns about Iraq (and Syria), the
parties agreed to refrain from joining or promoting any military or security coalition with a third party, "the objectives or
activities of which include launching aggression or other acts
of military hostility against the other Party." They also agreed
to refrain from "allowing the entry, stationing, and operating
on their territory, or through it, of military forces, personnel
or materiel of a third party, in circumstances which may adversely prejudice the security of the other Party."[44]

Although it addressed an Israeli concern, this component
of the treaty also served to formalize Israel's longstanding role
as a deterrent to the threat of Iraqi or Syrian military aggression against Jordan, a country situated along Israel's longest
and most vulnerable frontier. For decades, Israel had let it be
known that it would react to forestall the military incursion
of Jordan's powerful neighbors into the kingdom. In this regard, the treaty may not have been a novelty in the substantive
sense, but it did lend the added weight of a formal and public understanding that could hardly have gone unnoticed in
Damascus or Baghdad.

As for the kingdom's demographic anxieties, the Jordanians were eager to point out at the conclusion of the treaty
that, at long last, they had put to rest to the Jordan is Palestine idea; Israel had finally recognized the borders of the
Hashemite Kingdom. Indeed, the treaty noted in its General
Principles that the Parties "Further believe that within their
control, involuntary movements of persons in such a way as
to adversely prejudice the security of either Party should not
be permitted."[45] According to Prince Hassan, this signaled an
end to the "talk of Zionist expansion to the east of the River
Jordan and about obliterating the East Jordanian identity."[46]
(This provision was also designed to relieve Israeli anxieties
about a possible expulsion of Palestinians from Jordan to the
West Bank.) Hassan in fact met with the leader of the Israeli

Likud party, and future prime minister, Binyamin Netanyahu, in London twice before the signing of the peace treaty, in May and September 1994; he and King Hussein then met with Netanyahu again in Amman in December of that year. During each of these meetings, the Jordanians sought and received reassurance that the Likud did not support the Jordan is Palestine formula. At the same time, Netanyahu also assured the king and the crown prince that the Likud fully endorsed the peace treaty with Jordan and was committed to the kingdom's stability and integrity.[47] But despite all these assurances, Jordanian anxieties on this issue were never entirely put to rest and were easily revived in times of tension or uncertainty.

Finally, Jordan's interests in two of the issues left for final status negotiations between Israel and the Palestinians (scheduled to take place after implementing the transitional phase of the Oslo agreements) were explicitly recognized in the Jordan–Israel peace treaty. Signing the treaty *before* these negotiations commenced was intended to provide Jordan with greater leverage, through its partnership with Israel, over the determination of the future of the West Bank and Gaza.[48] First, the agreement reaffirmed Israeli respect for Jordan's special role in Jerusalem's Muslim shrines, already recognized in the Washington Declaration. This, according to one of Israel's key negotiators, provided a symbolic foothold for Jordan with regard to the final status negotiations in general.[49]

Second, it was agreed that Jordan would be party, in a framework to be negotiated, to final status discussions on the refugee issue, because Jordan had become the adopted home of most Palestinian refugees (now Jordanian citizens) outside historic Palestine. This agreement complemented the reaffirmation in the treaty that the fate of the refugees of 1967 would be addressed in a quadripartite committee of Israelis, Jordanians, Egyptians, and Palestinians as envisaged in the Oslo accords; the problem of the 1948 refugees had also been taken up by the Multilateral Working Group on Refugees established by the Madrid process. Jordan and Israel also agreed to implement UN and other international programs concerning refugees, "including assistance to their settlement."[50] In effect, this included the possible resettlement of refugees in Jordan, assuaging Israeli fears of a massive refugee return to Israel proper.

The Agreed Minutes of the treaty also recognized Jordan's economic interests in the West Bank, confirming that the two governments would deliberate with the aim of eliminating or mitigating any adverse effects on their economies.[51] Essentially, this was an Israeli undertaking to refrain from actions in the West Bank that might adversely effect the Jordanian economy. In fact, all Palestinian–Israeli final status issues were linked in one way or another to Jordanian interests (the border question could not help but affect Jordan directly, at least with reference to the ultimate dispensation of the Jordan Valley). Once Jordan's role had been formally recognized in two of the issues, it would be difficult to keep the kingdom from having input into the other issues as well, particularly if both parties agreed to the arrangement.

Above and beyond purely bilateral issues, the major strategic significance of the Israel–Jordan treaty derived from Jordan's relation to other states in the region and to the Palestinians. Israel had secured the formalization of Jordan's role as a stable buffer on the former's long and sensitive eastern front. Jordan, for its part, had established a solid platform of strategic understanding with Israel, from which it could protect its vital political and economic interests with relation to the emerging Palestinian entity well ahead of final status talks between Israelis and Palestinians. Israel had undertaken to give "high priority" to Jordan regarding the Muslim shrines in Jerusalem, to consult with the kingdom on its economic interests in the West Bank, and to commit itself to Jordan's demographic equilibrium. These were all gestures of Israeli goodwill emanating from a basic interest in the stability of the Hashemite Kingdom. Moreover, they reflected an Israeli proclivity to defer to Jordanian concerns on the Palestinian issue. King Hussein and Prime Minister Rabin had established not only a personal affinity, but a strategic rapport as well.

Notes

1. Asher Susser, "Jordan," *MECS*, vol. VI (1981–82), p. 677.

2. Susser, "Jordan," *MECS*, vol. I (1976–77), pp. 487–488.

3. Sa'id al-Tall, *Al-Urdunn wa-Filastin wa-mu'amarat al-watan al-badil* (Jordan and Palestine: the alternative homeland conspiracy) (Amman: Ministry of Culture and Youth, 1981).

4. Susser, "Jordan," *MECS*, vol. VI (1981–82), pp. 677–678; vol. VII (1982–83), p. 632.

5. *Le Figaro*, May 22, 1984.

6. Speech by Hussein on February 19, 1986, official Arabic text, pp. 16-21; Susser, "Jordan," *MECS*, vol. VIII (1983–84), p. 517; vol. X (1986), p. 451.

7. Jordan TV, July 30, in Federal Broadcasting Information Service *Daily Report–Near East and South Asia* (FBIS), August 2, 1989; Radio Amman, November 10, in FBIS, November 14, 1989; *Jordan Times*, October 19-20, 1989; *al-Hawadith*, October 27, 1989.

8. Lamis Andoni in *Middle East International*, February 2, 1990.

9. Jordan TV, June 17, in FBIS, June 19, 1990; Susser, "Jordan," *MECS*, vol. XIII (1989), p. 467; vol. XIV (1990), pp. 476–477.

10. *The Times*, March 26, 1984; Susser, "Jordan," *MECS*, vol. VIII (1983–84), p. 517; vol. X (1986), p. 451; vol. XV (1991), pp. 505–506.

11. Amatzia Baram, "Baathi Iraq and Hashemite Jordan: From Hostility to Alignment," *Middle East Journal* 45, no. 1 (Winter 1991), p. 65.

12. Hussein on Jordan TV, August 8, in FBIS, August 9, 1990; Hassan on Jordan TV, August 30, in FBIS, September 5, 1990.

13. Prime Minister Mudar Badran in *Jordan Times*, September 19, 1990.

14. *Ha'aretz*, August 19, *Jerusalem Post*, August 22, 31; *Middle East International*, September 28, 1990; Susser, "Jordan," *MECS*, vol. XIV (1990), p. 490; vol. XV (1991), p. 504.

15. Susser, "Jordan," *MECS*, vol. XIV (1990), pp. 488–490; vol. XV (1991), p. 504; Moshe Zak, *King Hussein Makes Peace: Thirty Years of Secret Talks* (in Hebrew) (Tel Aviv: Begin-Sadat Center for Strategic Studies, Bar Ilan University Press, 1996), pp. 47–51.

16. Zak, pp. 50-51.

17. *Ha'aretz*, February 20, 1991.

18. Zak, *King Hussein Makes Peace*, pp. 50–51; Susser, "Jordan," *MECS* vol. XV (1991), pp. 504–505.

19. *Jordan Times*, April 23, 1991.

20. *New York Times*, March 21, 1991.

21. James A. Baker with Thomas M. De Frank, *The Politics of Diplomacy:*

Revolution, War, and Peace, 1989–1992 (New York: Putnam, 1995), pp. 450–451; Susser, "Jordan," *MECS,* vol. XV (1991), pp. 512–513.

22. Susser, "Jordan," *MECS,* vol. XV (1991), p. 489.

23. Hussein in speeches to members of parliament and to officers of the armed forces, Jordan TV, July 9, 16, 1994, in FBIS, July 11, 18; *Al-Dustur,* July 17, 1994.

24. Susser, "Jordan," *MECS,* vol. XVIII (1994), p. 416.

25. George Hawatma in *Middle East International,* July 22, 1994.

26. Rami Khouri in *Jordan Times,* October 18, 1994; Susser, "Jordan," *MECS,* vol. XVIII (1994), p. 417.

27. Hussein in *Jordan Times,* May 24-25, 1991.

28. Radio Amman, May 9, in FBIS, May 10; *Jordan Times,* July 1, 1991; Susser, "Jordan," *MECS,* vol. XV (1991), pp. 505–506.

29. Hussein on Jordan TV, June 22, in FBIS, June 23, 1993; Majali on Jordan TV, August 25, in FBIS, August 26, 1993; Susser, "Jordan," *MECS,* vol. XVII (1993), pp. 468–469.

30. Conversation between the author and an advisor to Prince Hassan.

31. Musa al-Kaylani in *Jordan Times,* September 11 and October 9, 1993.

32. As quoted in the *Economist,* September 18, 1993, p. 23; Susser, "Jordan," *MECS,* vol. XVII (1993), p. 471.

33. *Al-Dustur,* August 24, October 13; *Jordan Times,* September 15; Jordan TV, September 18, November 9, 23, in FBIS, September 21, November 10, 24, 1993.

34. Susser, "Jordan," *MECS,* vol. XVII (1993), pp. 472–473.

35. *Economist,* June 11, 1994.

36. Radio Monte Carlo, June 23, in FBIS, June 24, 1994.

37. *Al-Hayat,* June 24, 1994.

38. Susser, "Jordan," *MECS,* vol. XVIII (1994), pp. 409–410.

39. Ibid.

40. Marwan Mu'asher, then-spokesman for the Jordanian delegation and current Jordanian ambassador to the United States, in conversation with the author.

41. *Ha'aretz,* July 11; Voice of Israel, July 14, in FBIS, July 14, 1994.

42. "The Washington Declaration (official text)," July 25, 1994.

43. Susser, "Jordan," *MECS,* vol. XVIII (1994), pp. 411–412.

44. State of Israel, "Treaty of Peace between the State of Israel and the Hashemite Kingdom of Jordan," October 26, 1994 (Ministry of Foreign Affairs, Jerusalem), Article 4.

45. Ibid., Article 2.

46. Radio Amman, October 20, in FBIS, October 21; Jordan TV, October 21, in FBIS, October 24; *Jordan Times,* October 22, 1994.

47. Susser, "Jordan," *MECS,* vol. XVIII (1994), p. 415.

48. Ibid., p. 419.

49. Conversation with the author.

50. State of Israel, "Treaty of Peace," Article 8. In the Arabic version of the treaty, the word used for settlement, *tawtin,* had always been understood to mean resettlement outside the refugees' original homes in Palestine, not repatriation.

51. Ibid., Agreed Minutes, p. 1.

Chapter 6
Jordan and the Aftermath of Peace

J ordanians let it be known on countless occasions, in public
statements and in talks with their Israeli, Palestinian, and
American counterparts, that they had vital interests in the
Palestinian question and in Israeli–Palestinian final status
negotiations, and they furthermore made their expectations
quite explicit. On December 4, 1997, in a publicized letter to
Prime Minister 'Abd al-Salam al-Majali, King Hussein elaborated on Jordan's Palestinian agenda, noting that none in
the Arab world had sacrificed more than the Hashemites had
for Palestine, and that Jordan's recognition of the Palestine
Liberation Organization's (PLO's) representative status in
1974 did not "spare [Jordan of] the moral and national responsibility" for dealing with the Palestinian question.
Moreover, Jordan's "pure national interest" was tied up in
each of the final status issues between Israelis and Palestinians: Jerusalem, refugees, borders, settlements, water, security,
and sovereignty. "The overlapping of Jordanian and Palestinian interests," the king concluded, made coordination with
the Palestinians imperative.[1] Of course, coordination with
Israel was equally crucial. (Hussein's involvement in the Israeli–Palestinian negotiations at Wye River in October 1998,
and his participation in the signing ceremony at the White
House that followed, were indicative of the special status to
which Jordan under King Hussein aspired.)

The formulation of the Jordanian position was, however,
crafted with much caution, so as to register Jordanian interest without appearing to encroach on the representative status
of Palestinian leadership. For instance, a clear-cut distinction
was made between a revival of the historic Hashemite role in

91

Palestine, which they explained was *not* their ambition, and the protection of Jordan's state interests, which was a legitimate concern of the kingdom.[2]

As Hussein reaffirmed in another letter to Prime Minister Majali in April 1998, Jordan would not compete with the PLO as the sole, legitimate representative of the Palestinian people, nor with the Palestinian Authority (PA) and Yasir 'Arafat as their spokesman. In fact, the king and other Jordanian spokesmen went to great lengths to assure the Palestinians that Jordan's own self-interest, not just abstract principle, dictated genuine Hashemite support for the PA. Any negative development in the West Bank, they argued, could have a spillover effect into Jordan with its own large Palestinian population. Jordan, therefore, would fully support the PA and the Palestinians until the establishment of their independent state on their national soil with its capital in Jerusalem.[3]

Jordan had no interest in half-measures that would not serve the cause of a stable solution and that might lead to some kind of Palestinian–Israeli confrontation. It therefore rejected partial Israeli withdrawal from Palestinian areas that would leave the Palestinians "squeezed into a limited space and thereby make it easier for the Israelis to get rid of them or control them."[4] The kingdom also had a vital interest in a lasting and mutually acceptable solution that would preclude "any attempt to change the map of the region."[5] The desired solution would affirm Jordanian Arab identity east of the Jordan River and Palestinian Arab identity to the west, culminating in the fulfillment of Palestinian aspirations to statehood. That, Prince Hassan concluded, would set "the final piece of the jigsaw [puzzle]" in place, defining the borders of Israel and providing the ultimate bulwark against any forced migration of Palestinians from the territory of Palestine.[6]

The bottom line of the Jordanian position was that the kingdom would not be a signatory to the final status agreements but would seek involvement to protect its own interests.[7] In the meantime, the Jordanians still had to clarify the "mechanism" that would ensure required coordination with Israel and the PA in the final status negotiations.[8] As for the longer term, Jordan's minister of information, Nasser Judeh, pointed out in November 1998 that there was a "real twinship (*tawa'ma*) between Jordan and Palestine."[9] Indeed the political, historical, and social bonds between the two peoples would make strategic ties essential to both sides once the Palestinians finally achieved their national aspirations.

Peace and the Protective Umbrella of the United States

Jordan's peace treaty with Israel not only provided a platform of potential strategic understanding between the two countries, it also meant "full rehabilitation" from the rift between Jordan and the United States that had occurred in the wake of the kingdom's pro-Iraqi Gulf War posture. This, in turn, added to Jordan's regional stature and paved the way for eventual reconciliation with Saudi Arabia and other Gulf states. But more important, although Iraq was still of great economic interest to Jordan, the peace treaty with Israel signified the culmination of Jordan's shift away from Iraq as the kingdom's "strategic hinterland." Iraq would now be replaced by the formal strategic protection of the United States and the informal protection of Israel against potential regional threats and rivalries that might originate in Syria, Iraq, or from the Palestinians.

As Jordan shifted away from Iraq in the post–Gulf War period, the United States enhanced its defense and economic commitment to the kingdom, while Israel increasingly lobbied on Jordan's behalf in the United States, urging the administration to accede to Jordanian economic and military requests. Joint U.S.–Jordanian military exercises were held regularly as of late 1992.[10] From the outset, however, it was clear to Jordan that debt relief and further military assistance from the United States would be commensurate with the kingdom's role in pushing the peace process forward between Israel and Jordan. For instance, in the wake of the Washington Declaration, and after debt relief legislation that was passed in Congress at an "unusually rapid pace," an agreement was reached in September 1994 on the phasing of debt relief to Jordan over a three-year period, in tandem with progress that the kingdom would make toward peace with Israel. Similarly, the United States undertook to supply Jordan with new military hardware, including F-16 aircraft that were only supplied after the conclusion of the Jordan–Israel peace treaty.[11]

As Jordan's historical associations with the United States were fully restored, many Jordanians felt that the kingdom had recovered its "natural place on the political map" and that they had finally broken out of their "bottleneck of isolation."[12] The rift between the kingdom and its traditional allies created by the Gulf War was, to a great extent, now a thing of the past. In his speech before the Jordanian parliament in October 1994 after the signing of the Jordan–Israel treaty, President Bill Clinton reaffirmed that the United States would meet Jordan's legitimate defense requirements by providing the security that the kingdom required.

The Jordanians had requested no less than $2.5 billion per annum over the course of ten years from the United States to revamp their military and revitalize their economy, but they almost certainly did not believe that they would receive this amount. All the same, they were disappointed by the level of aid they did receive and by the congressional hurdles they had to overcome, "hat in hand," before the U.S. commitment to debt relief was actually fulfilled. Aid to Jordan from the United States in various forms amounted to more than $375 million in 1995 (including $275 million to finance the debt relief). That amount has since been gradually increased, and the United States has also been instrumental in securing assistance for Jordan from the former's European allies as well as from the International Monetary Fund (IMF) and World Bank.

Disappointments with aid notwithstanding, the crucial point for Jordan was the fact that the United States continued to view the kingdom as a stable ally and linchpin of Middle Eastern security and stability. In November 1996, underscoring "the strategic relationship" binding the two countries,

Jordan was accorded the status of a major U.S. non-NATO ally.[13] Jordan's relations with the United States were now rock solid, and economic and military aid increased accordingly. Regular direct annual aid of $75 million was increased by $100 million (facilitated by a reduction of $50 million in aid each to Israel and Egypt) in 1997, and raised again to $225 million for 1998.[14] The last portion of Jordan's debt (of $700 million) to the United States was written off in September 1997, and after the signing of the Wye River agreement between Israel and the Palestinian Authority in October 1998, the United States pledged to provide Jordan with a further $300 million over three years.[15]

In the military sphere, Jordan received the first delivery of F-16 fighter aircraft in December 1997, which were added to other military hardware delivered at the end of 1996. Jordanian and U.S. forces meanwhile continued to conduct regular joint maneuvers in Jordan.[16] As Jordan entered the transition from Hussein to 'Abdallah II in February 1999, the United States was quick to offer increased political support and economic aid. President Clinton announced an additional $300 million package, two-thirds in military aid and the remaining $100 million in economic assistance. The move was designed in the immediate term to prevent a run on the Jordanian dinar, but stemmed more profoundly from the longstanding strategic commitment of the United States "to Jordan's well-being."[17] In the words of Defense Secretary William Cohen, the United States believed "that the economic stability and progress in Jordan is key to stability throughout the region."[18]

In his first visit to the United States as king in May 1999, 'Abdallah II, no doubt "preaching to the converted," continued to argue that Jordan was needed as a "fulcrum for the future stability of the region." He had no difficulty in obtaining further assurances of support for the kingdom's economic recovery from the administration and from Congress, as well as a presidential commitment to continue urging the G-7 industrial countries to relieve Jordan of its crushing debt burden.[19]

Jordan's Disappointment with the Israeli Peace Dividend

The peace treaty with Israel certainly produced the desired effect in terms of Jordan's relations with the United States. This was not the case, however, in the kingdom's relationship with Israel itself. In the run-up to the peace treaty and thereafter, King Hussein and Prime Minister Yitzhak Rabin developed an extraordinarily warm personal relationship and apparent strategic rapport, based on an Israeli appreciation of, and consideration for, Jordan's regional interests and vital concerns regarding the Palestinian question. After Rabin's assassination in November 1995, Israel's new prime minister, Shimon Peres, resumed close contact with Hussein, but these two did not enjoy the same level of rapport and mutual trust, and the instinctive warmth in the relationship soon dissipated.[20] In the aftermath of Israel's April 1996 Operation Grapes of Wrath in southern Lebanon, Peres's credibility in Jordan was said to have "reache[d] its nadir."[21] The Jordanians were reportedly infuriated not only by the extent of destruction wrought by this military campaign, but also by a number of other crucial components of Peres's regional policy that the kingdom's leadership found exasperating.

In fact, well before Grapes of Wrath, Jordanians were concerned that Israel's pursuit of an agreement with Syria might undermine Jordan's regional role. Subsequently, Israel's preference for Syria rather than Jordan as the key Arab intermediary for ending the campaign in Lebanon "was seen as a blow in the face that could hardly be tolerated."[22] But even more important, Jordanians were troubled by the possible impact that an emerging Palestinian entity could have on the kingdom and the stability of the Hashemite regime. The secret negotiations on final status issues between Yossi Beilin—representing the Israeli Labor party leadership—and Mahmud 'Abbas (Abu Mazen)—representing the PLO—in the absence of consultation or coordination with Jordan were not well received in the kingdom. Instead, these talks were seen as "clearly disregarding Jordan's strategic interests in the West Bank"[23] and conflicting with statements that had been made by then–Foreign Minister Ehud Barak on Jordan's key role in a permanent settlement with the Palestinians.[24]

Furthermore, Jordan had developed exaggerated expectations of the economic advantages—the "dividends of peace"—it would enjoy as a result of its political and geographic location. These expectations included the belief that the kingdom's geographic location and unique interaction with Palestine would transform Jordan into a bridge for Israel's future integration into the region. Transport and transit trade would increase, and the West Bank market would provide for the rapid growth of Jordan's exports. In the longer term, new investment by Arab, foreign, and local investors in what should be a more secure environment would ensure economic development for the kingdom.[25] Despite these hopes, little of this vision had materialized in the first few years of peace with Israel.

Jordanian officials complained that Peres had spoken much about the economic underpinnings of peace while Israel had in fact implemented policies that were overprotective of Israeli business interests. The Jordanians accordingly concluded that the Israeli market would not be a likely substitute for declining trade with Iraq. Prince Hassan referred to the "shackled economy" of the West Bank and Gaza, to which Jordan exported some $20 million worth of goods annually, far less than Israel's exports to these areas (some $2 billion) and far below Jordanian expectations. Jordan also accused Israel of imposing unnecessary restrictions on Jordanian trade to preserve the Palestinian areas as a captive market for Israeli products.[26]

Given their criticism of Peres, the Jordanians were not particularly dismayed by his defeat in Israel's May 1996 elections.[27] In fact, the official Jordanian response to Binyamin Netanyahu's election victory was singularly complacent, as opposed to the immediate alarm expressed in much of the rest of the Arab world. The Jordanian leadership may have even expected Netanyahu's tougher negotiating stance toward the Palestinians to result in greater Israeli consideration for Jordanian interests in this crucial domain. But Jordanian anxieties regarding Netanyahu began to surface, and they were soon to become concerned about the consequences of an Israeli–Palestinian impasse. Commentators in Jordan referred to Netanyahu as a "slippery politician . . . telling all his different interlocutors what they want[ed] to hear."[28] Netanyahu had to understand, they argued, that Jordan could not be taken for granted. The continuation of warm peace was not a realistic option if there were an impasse on other tracks.[29] As long as the Jordanians believed in Netanyahu's willingness and capacity to continue the peace process, they urged restraint on their fellow Arabs to forestall an overreaction that might force Netanyahu into a defensive and uncompromising posture. But once their confidence in the Israeli premier had eroded, Jordanian tactics changed dramatically. Ever-increasing pressure was brought to bear on Netanyahu to produce the tangible progress that Jordanians felt was absolutely essential to protect their own domestic and inter-Arab interests.

Matters came to a head in late September 1996, following Israel's decision to open a new exit to the Hasmonean tunnel in Jerusalem and the subsequent outbreak of violent clashes between Israelis and Palestinians. It was at this point that Jordanian–Israeli relations entered their worst crisis since the signing of the peace treaty, although King Hussein joined Netanyahu and Arafat at an early October summit convened by President Clinton in Washington in an effort to get the peace process back on track. At the summit, Hussein was unusually direct in his devastating criticism of Netanyahu. During interviews with the media he was less abrupt, but his lack of confidence in Netanyahu was obvious as he accused Israel of fueling militancy by failing to honor its agreements with the Palestinians. The Jordanians were making it clear to Israel that they could not accept deadlock in the Israeli–Palestinian negotiations. They furthermore rejected Israel's settlement policy as posing not only "the gravest danger" to the peace process, but also a direct threat to the kingdom's own security and stability.[30]

This Jordanian apprehension about security was based on the rekindled fear that Israeli policy might eventually lead to a displacement of Palestinians to make room for new Israeli settlements, or, alternatively, provoke a violent Palestinian–Israeli conflict. A flare-up of such violence, it was feared, might trigger a Palestinian exodus that would spill over into the kingdom and inspire a revival in Israel of the dreaded Jordan is Palestine theory.[31] Because of its "geographic and cultural proximity to Palestine," Prince Hassan once said, Jordan did not have the luxury of "isolating [itself] from the economic and political pressures generated in the Palestinian territories."[32] The kingdom therefore supported stability in the West Bank, as it "did not want to have to deal with a fourth wave of refugees."[33]

Shortly after the eruption of the Har Homa/Jabal Abu Ghunaym crisis in early 1997, Hussein sent two unusually strong-worded messages to Netanyahu. The first was sent on February 26, before the Israeli government's decision to go ahead with the construction project there, warning against the negative repercussions of such a decision. In the second message, sent on March 9, the king expressed his deep and genuine distress "over the accumulating tragic actions" that Netanyahu had initiated, making peace "appear more and more like a distant, elusive mirage. . . . You cannot send me assurances that you would not sanction any further construction of settlements . . . and then renege on your commitment."[34] The king went on to accuse Netanyahu of seeking to humiliate the Palestinians through Israel's settlement policy and the relatively minor further redeployment offered at the time.[35]

Hussein was troubled enough on this occasion to restate longstanding Jordanian anxieties about the forcible creation by Israel of an "alternative homeland" for the Palestinians in Jordan, and he expressed the fear that Israeli policies were deliberately designed to maneuver the Palestinians "into inevitable violent resistance." This, in turn, could eventually result in a major confrontation, "creating yet a fresh exodus of hapless Palestinians" from their homeland. "How can I work with you as a partner and true friend in this confused and confusing atmosphere when I sense an intent to destroy all I have worked to build between our peoples and states?"[36]

Jordanian–Israeli relations were henceforth governed by a measure of tension. The Jordanians frequently complained about Israeli policies, blaming the Netanyahu government for the stalemate in the peace process on both the Palestinian and the Syrian tracks. In April 1998, one day after an unsuccessful meeting with Netanyahu in Eilat, Hussein sent another letter to the Israeli premier warning that the current stalemate could endanger the entire region, which faced the prospect of being engulfed by "an era of darkness" if the peace process failed.[37] Netanyahu exasperated Hussein. The king complained that the peace process was faltering because Rabin's departure had "changed the equation." Moreover, Hussein observed, the Arabs and Israelis had seemingly changed places. Once it was the Arabs who engaged in empty talk detached from reality, provoking the entire world against them. It seemed that "the opposite [was] now true."[38]

One Jordanian commentator suggested that the negative positions adopted by the Israeli government would not undermine Jordan's commitment to the peace treaty, but they would affect the warmth of the relationship between the two countries. In this scenario, coexistence would eventually become no more than a "cold peace" representing the bare minimum in bilateral ties, and Jordan's only real option would be to reinforce relations with its Arab hinterland.[39] As Prime Minister Fayiz Tarawina (who replaced 'Abd al-Salam al-Majali in August 1998) remarked, Jordan's treaty with Israel did not necessitate the abandonment of the kingdom's Arab identity.[40]

Israel, the Arab Hinterland, and the Swing of the Strategic Pendulum

The crisis of confidence between Hussein and Netanyahu had a corrosive effect on at least one foundation of Jordan's rationale of peace with Israel: that their mutual relations could be used as a means of achieving "an influential role in overall peacemaking in the Arab world," especially on the Palestinian track.[41]

As the strategic understanding with Israel eroded, Jordan's attitude toward Iraq accordingly began to shift. Despite expressions of discontent with Saddam Hussein's regime, Jordan increasingly sought to normalize relations with Iraq. Disappointment with the economic dividends of peace with Israel was an added incentive for the kingdom to seek out new trade deals with Iraq, and consequently, Jordanians began to tone down their anti-Iraq rhetoric in preparation to benefit from new trading opportunities. When the Iraqis finally decided in May 1996 to accept United Nations (UN) Security Council resolution 986 allowing for oil exports to finance food imports, Jordan welcomed the decision. The Iraqis, for their part, still dependent on the kingdom as their most secure tether to the outside world, had been unusually restrained in their reaction to Jordan's undoing of their alliance in the wake of the Gulf War.

Jordan's policy shift was not entirely detached from domestic constraints, as peace with Israel had given rise to a serious identity debate in Jordanian intellectual circles. Among the ultra-Jordanian (anti-Palestinian) nationalists, some contended that Jordan's regional importance did not derive primarily from its involvement with the Palestinians (and/or Israel), but rather from the kingdom's geopolitical centrality and its ties to Syria and Iraq. These arguments corresponded with the position of many Arab nationalists and Islamists in Jordan, who were of the opinion that the peace accord with Israel had isolated the country from its natural Arab–Islamic neighbors. The peace, they contended, came in the context of a new "Middle Easternism" (*sharq awsatiyya*) of which Israel was a legitimate part, thereby eroding Jordan's Arab identity and overemphasizing the kingdom's dependence on Israel and the United States. These kinds of arguments served an Iraqi orientation, not to mention the self-interest of the influential economic lobby and Saddam's continued personal popularity in Jordan.

Perhaps with such considerations in mind, King Hussein began to strike a new balance between Jordan's desire to see Iraq return to the Arab fold and its continued interest in preserving and promoting the peace with Israel. Jordan's more conciliatory tone deviated only temporarily in August 1996 when the Jordanian government accused the Iraqis of being involved in bread riots that took place in southern Jordan that month. These recriminations did not last for long, however, and just weeks later, Jordan officially expressed disapproval of the American missile strikes against Iraq, denounced external interference in Iraq's domestic affairs, and again criticized U.S. dual containment policy.

More significantly, Crown Prince Hassan now began to speak of the need for a regional security network that would not exclude Iraq, citing Jordan's "new worries about Israel."[42] This was not an isolated statement. In the context of a discussion of Jordanian anxieties about Israel, King Hussein subsequently observed that a threatened and weak Iraq was an added burden on the Arabs and constituted an unacceptable situation that should not be allowed to persist.[43]

Initial signs of reconciliation with Iraq became more pronounced during much of 1997. Iraqi deputy prime minister Tariq 'Aziz met regularly with senior Jordanian officials in Amman, including Hussein and Hassan. Jordan continued to receive all its oil supplies (4.5 million tons of crude oil and oil derivatives in 1997 and 4.8 million tons in 1998) from Iraq—partly free of charge and partly at preferential cost both in exchange for goods and in partial repayment of the Iraqi debt to Jordan. Trade between the two countries picked up as did the use of the Aqaba port for increased imports to Iraq in the wake of the UN "oil for food" arrangement.[44]

In regional affairs, the Jordanian government—and even more so the press, parliament, and political parties of every branch—invariably supported Iraq. Jordanians criticized the Turkish incursion into northern Iraq in May 1997 as potentially threatening to the regional state order. Calling for a Turkish withdrawal, Hussein expressed his concern regarding designs to infringe upon Iraq's territorial integrity and to redraw the map of the region.[45]

In March 1997, Prime Minister 'Abd al-Salam al-Majali publicly took exception to a statement by Secretary of State Madeleine Albright to the effect that Saddam had to be removed as a precondition for dialogue with Iraq. Majali described the U.S. position as an unacceptable interference in Iraq's domestic affairs.[46] Jordan similarly made it quite clear that it would not be party to any international effort to unseat the Iraqi regime. In July 1997, the radio station of the Iraqi National Accord Movement was also reported to have ceased broadcasting from within Jordan, which curtailed the other activities of Iraqi opposition groups in the kingdom.[47] (The May 1997 signing of a "working program" between the Iraqi Ba'th and the Jordanian Islamic Action Front had constituted Iraqi retaliation against Jordan's meddling in Iraqi domestic affairs).[48]

Jordan did urge Iraq to comply with all UN resolutions and to facilitate the UN Special Commission (UNSCOM) inspections. But the Jordanians, who now spoke of the need to rehabilitate Iraq and to restore its regional role, also lobbied the United States, Britain, and other countries for the removal of the sanctions on Iraq and publicly opposed the use of force against the Iraqis.[49] When a crisis over the inspections loomed on the horizon in November 1997, Jordan called for dialogue between the United States and Iraq and "categorically . . . denounce[d] any military action against Iraq."[50] The Jordanians, who took some credit for the diplomatic solution and subsequently earned public Iraqi appreciation for their "mediating role," therefore welcomed an agreement to which Hussein contributed through intensive talks with the United States and Britain and that temporarily defused the standoff between Iraq and the UN.[51]

Given its actions on Iraq's behalf, Jordan was shocked by the December 1997 Iraqi execution of four Jordanian nationals for minor smuggling offenses. King Hussein denounced this "heinous crime," noting that he was incapable of figuring out "the thinking, the logic, the mental process" governing Saddam's actions.[52] Jordan withdrew its chargé d'affaires from Baghdad and ordered the expulsion of seven Iraqi diplomats from Amman. The Iraqis subsequently spared a fifth Jordanian facing similar smuggling charges and after no more than a few days, the "heinous crime" was deflated in Jordanian parlance to merely an "unfortunate development" that would not affect bilateral ties between the two countries.[53] Much to Jordan's disappointment and frustration, however, relations with Iraq continued in the pattern of unpredictable irregularity.

In January 1998, in what appeared to be a gesture of good-will, the Iraqis released a few dozen Jordanians who had been imprisoned in Iraqi jails. The Jordanian government took credit for this development as well, as an outcome of the efforts of King Hussein and Crown Prince Hassan. But the Iraqis had actually allowed the release in response to a personal request by none other than the most outspoken figure of Jordan's Islamist opposition, the maverick Layth Shubaylat. Indeed, Iraqi officials pointedly released the prisoners "in honor of the fraternal Jordanian people," and not in deference to the Jordanian government. As if to add insult to injury, the Iraqis sent the prisoners home in a convoy led by Shubaylat's car. Thus, what might have been a friendly gesture under other circumstances was hardly so in this case. On the contrary, it was a patently deliberate gesture of ill will, an expression of Iraqi displeasure with Jordan's ties to the Iraqi opposition, and a form of retaliation for Jordan's tendency to express support for the Iraqi people rather than for Saddam's regime. Apparently, this was Saddam's way of saying that Iraq could, and would, do just the same to Jordan.[54]

Shortly thereafter, the specter of renewed military confrontation between Iraq and the United States aroused both anxiety and extreme frustration with Iraq in the kingdom. Jordanians especially feared an inundation of refugees fleeing war-torn Iraq. (There were already more than 100,000 Iraqis in Jordan, and the Jordanians had their hands full policing their border with Iraq to curb smuggling and infiltration.[55]) They were also concerned that a possible interruption in their conveniently inexpensive oil imports from Iraq would compel them to turn to alternative, and much more expensive, suppliers.

Since the beginning of their efforts to forge a renewed rapprochement with Iraq, the Jordanians had charted a cautious middle course. They did not support military action against Iraq and consistently called for the lifting of sanctions. But at the same time, Jordan criticized Iraqi evasive tactics on weapons inspections and urged Iraqi compliance with UN resolutions—"full and to-the-letter implementation," as Hussein put it, including cooperation with the UNSCOM observers.[56]

Thus, when the United States and Iraq faced yet another standoff in January–February 1998, there was a discernible pro-American (or anti-Iraqi) tilt in the Jordanian position. On the one hand, Jordan appealed to the United States to refrain from the use of force and informed the Americans that the kingdom would not allow its airspace to be used for attacks against Iraq. Jordan was similarly said to have warned Israel to refrain from retaliating against Iraq by overflying Jordanian territory. But on the other hand, the Jordanian government (as opposed to the Jordanian press, including the partially government-owned dailies that generally supported Iraq unequivocally) did not fail to mention Iraq's own responsibility for the crisis, stemming from its lack of cooperation with UNSCOM.[57]

King Hussein, in a publicized letter to Crown Prince Hassan at the end of January, warned Saddam of the serious consequences that would follow a repeat of his political Gulf War miscalculation. Hussein expressed understanding for the U.S. position, arguing that the international community could not be expected to allow any country to defy UN Security Council resolutions. Jordan clearly preferred that a diplomatic solution to the crisis be achieved through the Security Council, the king noted, but he appreciated the U.S. position that if this avenue proved fruitless, no alternative would remain but the resort to force in order to prevent a state that had already used weapons of mass destruction from continuing to develop them.[58]

Hussein was clearly exasperated by the vagaries of the Iraqi leadership. He had told the Iraqi foreign minister, Muhammad Sa'id al-Sahhaf, in the midst of this crisis that if the Iraqis had only been people of their word, Iraq could have returned to normalcy long ago—to the benefit not only of the Iraqi people but of Iraq's neighbors as well, which were forced to suffer the consequences of Iraqi folly and irresponsibility.[59] In the meantime, the Jordanians made every effort to avert a military confrontation,[60] and when a diplomatic solution to the crisis was reached in late February, they were genuinely relieved—for domestic political reasons as much as for the sake of regional security and economic interests.

Still, the anti-Iraqi tilt in Jordan's official position was not popular with domestic public opinion. Although the authorities banned all rallies, demonstrations in support of Iraq were staged in Amman in mid-February 1998, followed by violent protests and clashes with security forces in the southern town of Ma'an.[61] The Jordanians had no interest in driving their relations with Iraq to the brink, and in the aftermath of the February crisis, the government was quick to resume its middle course. Jordan, according to Prince Hassan, was keen on maintaining relations with the Iraqis, based on the assessment that "we [the Jordanians] need them for support as much as they need us for the same purpose."[62]

The government also rejected the suggestion that the Iraqis might have instigated the Ma'an incidents,[63] and King Hussein, noting that the American demand for Saddam's ouster was "unacceptable," revived his proposal (from the previous standoff between the United States and Iraq in November 1997) that the two countries enter into a dialogue. The king had no illusions about the willingness of the Iraqis to actually commit themselves "to certain things that some people are trying to avoid." Even so, direct dialogue, he contended, was the only way to exit the cycle of recurring crises and work toward the eventual achievement of full and unconditional Iraqi implementation of its international commitments, the preservation of Iraqi territorial integrity, and the lifting of sanctions.[64]

But King Hussein's sentiments toward the Iraqi regime remained ambivalent. He made no secret of the fact that he had considerable difficulty in dealing with Saddam, a fact that seemed to suggest that he would have preferred someone else at the helm of his powerful neighboring state. The two leaders had not spoken since the 1990 crisis, and the king was in any case incapable of getting Saddam to accept Jordan's right to expect consideration for Jordanian interests when Iraq adopted policies that had ramifications for the region as a whole. Jordan supported the Iraqi people ("I say people," the king emphasized), adding that he hoped one day to see mutual understanding at the leadership level as well. All the same, King Hussein maintained, as long as Saddam remained in power, the Iraqi leader had to be dealt with.[65]

Relations with Iraq seemed genuinely to be improving when Iraqi foreign minister Sahhaf visited Jordan for three days in mid-May 1998 for talks with Hussein, Hassan, and other Jordanian leaders. Sahhaf conveyed a message from Saddam to the king designed to encourage Jordan to continue its efforts at promoting U.S.–Iraqi dialogue and having sanctions removed.[66] His visit had the desired effect, and shortly thereafter, Prime Minister Majali declared that the theory according to which the starving of the Iraqi people would result in the overthrow of the regime in Baghdad was wrong. In July, a new Jordanian ambassador was sent to Baghdad, after approximately a year in which Jordan had only been represented there by a chargé d'affaires. Concurrently, a palpable decline was reported in the activities of the Amman-based Iraqi opposition to the point that operatives had begun to leave Jordan altogether.[67]

The revived on again–off again rapprochement, however, had barely taken root when it was upset yet again. Jordanian efforts to have the Iraqis come clean with the UN on the issue of weapons of mass destruction (about which the Jordanians naturally had their own anxieties) were not fruitful, and by late 1998, the United States and the Iraqis were in the throes of another crisis. The Jordanians, surprised and disillusioned yet again, this time by the Iraqi decision to cease cooperation with UNSCOM, could hardly conceal their annoyance. They continued to appeal for a diplomatic solution to the crisis, but their criticism of Iraq was obvious.[68] As Foreign Minister ʻAbd al-Ilah al-Khatib stated, the Jordanians found Iraq's proclivity to plunge headlong into one crisis after another to be incomprehensible.[69] The Iraqis were alienating even their potentially more friendly neighbors.

Despite the continued popular solidarity with Iraq in Jordan, Jordanian displeasure at the official level was amplified at the meeting of the Arab Parliamentary Union (APU) held in Amman in late December 1998. The Iraqis did not hesitate to make their expectations of the APU abundantly clear well in advance, noting that "a centrist position" would not suffice and that nothing short of "resolutions denouncing the aggression" of the United States and Britain would be acceptable.[70]

Much to their dismay, however, Crown Prince Hassan, acting as regent in Hussein's absence, chose to ignore the Iraqi directive. In a veiled critique of Western powers during his keynote address to the conference, he suggested that the use of force should be a last resort. He refrained, however, from actually condemning the U.S. and British air strikes against Iraq. Hassan confined his remarks to little more than an empathic expression of solidarity with the Iraqi people, and a reiteration of Jordan's longstanding support for the territorial integrity of Iraq, the removal of sanctions, and the return of Iraq to the Arab fold. Nevertheless, since Jordan had a genuine interest in a regional equilibrium that included a stable, prosperous, and friendly Iraqi hinterland, Hassan made it equally clear that there could be no real peace and security in the region without Iraq.[71]

These pleasantries, although sincere, fell far short of Iraqi expectations. The Iraqis were enraged by Hassan's distinction between the Iraqi people and their government, and even more so by his allusions to the plight of Kuwaiti prisoners held in Iraq and the general need to protect human rights there.[72] The Jordanians then added insult to injury by banning a scheduled meeting during the APU between the speaker of the Iraqi parliament and members of the Jordanian professional associations and opposition parties who were all strongly supportive of Iraq.

Jordanian–Iraqi relations had sunk to yet another low, and their unsteady association was accompanied by a decline in the volume of bilateral trade. The continued sanctions prevented an Iraqi economic recovery, which could have provided for a concomitant rise in demand for Jordanian imports by Iraq. The Jordanians also faced increasing competition from other Middle Eastern states for the restricted Iraqi market, and low oil prices made it even more difficult for Iraq to prevent a further reduction of imports from Jordan.

With relations again in decline, the Iraqis were not sorry to see King Hussein summarily depose Hassan from his position as crown prince in January 1999. They were also demonstratively unmoved by the king's passing the following month. As opposed to most other countries, the Iraqis made no official comment and dispatched a relatively low-level official to the king's funeral.[73] Iraq's public references to Jordan's new king, 'Abdallah II, varied initially from derision to indifference. Needless to say, 'Abdullah's whirlwind tour of Arab and other countries shortly after his ascension to the throne did not include Iraq.

Although Iraq and Jordan remained economically dependent on each other, and neither sought any form of confrontation, the vagaries and unpredictability of Saddam's regime were constantly perplexing irritants in the Jordanian–Iraqi relationship. King 'Abdallah reassured the Iraqis and informed the United States that Jordan would not participate in any effort to unseat Saddam or attack Iraq,[74] and the

Iraqis, for their part, still supplied Jordan with all its oil requirements at concessionary prices. But the volume of bilateral trade continued to decline in 1999,[75] and all in all, political and economic ties with Iraq were a steadily less attractive proposition for Jordan. This was particularly the case after Jordan's rapprochement with the United States, Saudi Arabia, and Kuwait—all the more so as long as low oil prices continued to restrict Iraqi purchasing power.

Broken Reeds in Baghdad and Damascus

By the end of the 1990s, Jordan's uncertain relationship with Iraq had become more of a liability than an asset. Moreover, the rift with Syria made it impossible for the kingdom to maneuver between its neighbors—as it had so often been able to do in the past—compensating for the difficult relationship with Iraq by improving ties with Damascus. Indeed, Jordanian efforts to ease tensions with Syria had come to naught as Syrian hostility toward Jordan since the signing of the kingdom's peace treaty with Israel in 1994 not only persisted but had become even more acerbic.

The Syrians repeatedly aired their grievances about the Jordan–Israel relationship that existed, they contended, "at the expense of Arab rights." Jordan's own involvement in Iraqi affairs was another cause for Syrian aggravation and apprehension, and Jordan's close ties with Turkey only made matters worse, arousing Syrian fears of pro-American encirclement.[76] Syria's displeasure with Jordan's regional policies may have been one of the reasons for a certain improvement in Syrian–Iraqi relations in the late-1990s, which, in turn, further curtailed Jordan's room to maneuver in the region. Jordanian assurances that their country would never be party to any military alliance against another Arab state and that their cooperation with Turkey was unrelated to Israel made no impact whatsoever on the Syrians. They continued to suspect Jordanian–Israeli–Turkish collusion at every turn and to intimidate the Jordanians by aiding and abetting subversive activities against the kingdom.

In May 1998, the two countries reaffirmed in principle their 1987 agreement to jointly construct the Wahda Dam on the Yarmuk River (the project was expected to cost more than $400 million, the sources for which had yet to be discovered). But this had no apparent effect on bilateral relations, which continued to deteriorate. Saudi efforts to mediate between Amman and Damascus proved fruitless as the Jordanians refused to accede to Syrian pressure to downscale relations with Israel as a precondition for reconciliation.[77]

In September 1998, Turkish premier Mesut Yilmaz paid an official visit to Amman, which was presumably seen in Damascus as an insufferable provocation. Shortly thereafter, Turkey mounted military pressure to coerce the Syrians into ceasing their support for the Kurdish nationalists in conflict with the Turks. Having arrived at the ostensibly logical conclusion that Jordan might collude with Turkey and Israel against Syria, the Syrians now launched a particularly vicious propaganda tirade against Jordan, the likes of which the Jordanians had not experienced for years. Led by none other than Syrian minister of defense Mustafa Tlas, a man with a penchant for coarse rhetoric, the Syrian campaign included diminutive references to Jordan as "southern Syria" and accused the Jordanians of historical treachery against the Arab cause.[78] The Jordanians naturally rejected this allegation and responded by condemning Syria for the inhumane mistreatment of hundreds of Jordanian nationals, including government officials, who were said to be missing there or held in Syrian jails, mostly without trial.[79]

Jordanian intercession with the Turks to reduce tension with Syria and encourage the resort to a peaceful resolution of differences failed to appease the Syrians.[80] Syria, after all, had reason to be dissatisfied with the Jordanian position on the crisis, which stopped far short of siding with the Syrians against Turkey and even demonstrated sympathy for the Turks as victims of Kurdish terrorism.[81] But Jordan had little to gain from prolonged estrangement with Syria and was quite willing to mend fences, especially as relations with Iraq and with the

Netanyahu government in Israel were both fraught with such difficulty. Before such reconciliation was possible, however, the Jordanians expected Syria to cease its negative media campaign against the kingdom, abstain from meddling in Jordanian security and domestic affairs, and release Jordanian detainees held in Syria without trial.[82] Jordan and Syria continued to exchange vitriolic insults, and until Hussein's death there was little to show in the way of rapprochement between the two.[83]

The Tenuous Syrian Option

At a time when ties with Israel were uncertain, Iraq was behaving in a typically unpredictable manner, and relations with Syria were frigid, Jordan found itself in a situation of extraordinary strategic discomfort which gave rise to a sense of political suffocation. It would come as no surprise, then, that as soon as a real chance for improving relations with Syria became an option—after King Hussein's death—the Jordanians seized upon it. Restored relations with Syria, as with Iraq, had an important domestic dimension, especially for a new king seeking to establish his credentials in the eyes of his subjects. Strengthening ties with Syria, or even with Iraq, had the added value of deflecting criticism from the Arab nationalist or Islamist opposition, which suggested that peace with Israel came at the expense of Jordan's Arab identity and the country's natural ties with the Arab world. In any case, from the regime's point of view, relations with the Arab hinterland and Israel were in no way mutually exclusive.

The dramatic and unexpected participation of President Hafiz al-Asad in Hussein's funeral, his private talks with freshly installed King 'Abdallah II, and the public Syrian commitment to Jordan's stability and security turned a new leaf in Jordanian–Syrian relations. For the first time in a decade, Jordan could once again enjoy the immediate relief afforded by what had traditionally been its room to maneuver between Syria and Iraq. Quite ironically, Hussein's death, dreaded for so long as a potentially destabilizing factor, served in practice to draw attention to Jordan's geopolitical centrality. This recognition tended to urge everyone, including decision makers in Damascus, to ensure continued stability in the kingdom and a smooth transition from Hussein to 'Abdallah II, lest any of Jordan's other neighbors derive undue advantage from Jordanian weakness.

For Syria, Hussein's departure from the scene was also a face-saving opportunity to "let bygones be bygones." With Israel in the throes of an election campaign in which the possible renewal of negotiations with Syria figured prominently, the Syrian–Jordanian rapprochement allowed the Syrians to improve their standing in Washington and to prepare for either a new government in Jerusalem or for the reelection of Netanyahu. In the first case, Jordan could serve a useful purpose as a conduit of communication between Jerusalem and Damascus in the negotiations likely to ensue; in the second, the kingdom could serve as an ally pressuring Israel for change.

As Jordan and Syria entered a new era of political coordination and economic cooperation, 'Abdallah visited Damascus in April and was accorded an especially warm welcome. But this honeymoon did not represent an immediate revival of the intimacy that characterized relations between Asad and Hussein in the mid-1970s. The Jordanians remained ever cautious of Syria's domineering proclivities and spoke recurrently of relations "set on an equal footing."[84] Yet, the evolving relationship did include assurances by Damascus that it had come to terms with Jordan's peace treaty with Israel. Jordan reciprocated with reassurances that Syria had nothing to fear from the kingdom's relations with either Israel or Turkey. As the Jordanians liked to say, their peace treaty with Israel was a strategic option from which it would not turn back; but at the same time, it would "have no bearing whatsoever on the kingdom's Arab identity."[85]

Since Jordan's relations with Israel and Syria were not a zero-sum game, King 'Abdallah did not hesitate to try his hand at facilitating the resumption of Israeli–Syrian negotiations by assisting the parties in establishing an agreed-upon point of departure for renewed talks.[86] The Syrians were also ready for symbolic gestures of goodwill, and they agreed to assist Jordan with the kingdom's urgent water shortage. But Jordan and Syria had other good reasons for collaboration: the Jordanians were quite willing to recognize Syria's interests in Lebanon in exchange for Syrian recognition of Jordan's Palestinian interests. Furthermore, both states shared concerns about Israel and Iraq, not to mention their shared suspicion and mistrust of Yasir 'Arafat.

The rapprochement was pursued with caution. The Syrians were always treated with circumspection, yet relations between Syria and Jordan were being upgraded. 'Abdallah maintained close contact with Asad, as well as with Asad's son and possible successor, Bashar, a contemporary of 'Abdallah and of a similar Western educational background. Talks were resumed for constructing the Wahda Dam; joint economic committees, defunct for a decade, were revived; top-level officials exchanged regular visits; and finally, in July 1999, within the framework of general amnesty in Syria, many of the Jordanian prisoners held there were released.

The renewal of the Syrian option served to underscore the historical pattern: Jordan invariably sought to secure relations with at least one of its more powerful neighbors—Israel, Syria, Iraq, or Saudi Arabia—at any given time. The less receptive the Iraqis were to Jordanian overtures, the more Jordan tended to actively pursue understandings with other Arab states and/or Israel. In this case, Jordan had turned toward the Syrians.

Notes

1. Radio Amman, December 4, 1997, as published in Federal Broadcasting Information Service *Daily Report–Near East and South Asia* (FBIS) online (date listed for FBIS online citations is original date of publication).

2. Eg. Prime Minister Tarawina in *al-Dustur,* October 17; Joint Jordanian-Israeli statement, Jordan News Agency–Petra (JNA) (FBIS online), November 24, 1998.

3. Jordan TV (FBIS online), April 15, May 20, 1998.

4. Deputy Prime Minister Jawad al-'Anani in *al-Ittihad* (FBIS online), August 14, 1998.

5. Hassan on Jordan TV, August 6 (FBIS online); Deputy Prime Minister Jawad al-'Anani in *al-Ittihad* (FBIS online), August 14, 1998.

6. Jordan TV (FBIS online), October 29, 1998.

7. Summary of press conference given by Prime Minister 'Abd al-Ra'uf al-Rawabda, August 9, 1999, in *Jordan Focus* (online) "Special: Jordan," August 10, 1999.

8. *Al-Dustur*, December 15, 1998.

9. *Al-Dustur*, November 7, 1998.

10. Asher Susser, "Jordan," *MECS*, vol. XVI (1992), p. 561; vol. XVII (1993), pp. 479–480; vol. XIX (1995), p. 421; vol. XX (1996), p. 448.

11. Susser, "Jordan," *MECS*, vol. XVIII (1994), pp. 409–410, 431.

12. Musa al-Kaylani in *Jordan Times*, October 29, 1994; Susser, "Jordan," *MECS*, vol. XVIII (1994), p. 419.

13. Susser, "Jordan," *MECS*, vol. XVIII (1994), p. 431; vol. XIX (1995), p. 421; vol. XX (1996), p. 449.

14. *Ha'aretz*, May 16, 18; *al-Ra'y*, May 17; *Jordan Times*, June 8, 18, October 30–31, November 4, 1997.

15. For more on the writing off of Jordan's debt, see *Jordan Times*, April 3–4; Radio Amman (FBIS online), September 25, 1997.

16. *Jordan Times*, March 11, May 24, June 12–13, 1997.

17. A senior adviser to President Clinton, as quoted in the *Washington Post*, February 6, 1999.

18. *Jordan Times*, March 11, 1999.

19. *Jordan Times*, May 18, 22; *Washington Post*, May 18, 1999.

20. Susser, "Jordan," *MECS*, vol. XIX (1995), pp. 404–405.

21. Susser, "Jordan," *MECS*, vol. XX (1996), p. 436.

22. Samir Mutawi in *Jordan Times*, May 29, 1996.

23. Ibid.

24. Susser, "Jordan," *MECS*, vol. XX (1996), pp. 435–436.

25. Susser, "Jordan," *MECS*, vol. XVIII (1994), pp. 418–419.

26. *Al-Ahram, al-Dustur*, December 3, 1998.

27. Susser, "Jordan," *MECS*, vol. XX (1996), p. 436.

28. Rami Khouri and Musa al-Kaylani in *Jordan Times*, August 6, September 21, 1996.

29. Susser, "Jordan," *MECS*, vol. XX (1996), p. 438.

30. Ibid., p. 440.

31. *Jordan Times*, June 20-21, July 13, 1996.

32. *Jordan Times*, June 20-21, 1996.

33. *Jordan Times*, November 24, 1996; Susser, "Jordan," *MECS*, vol. XX (1996), p. 437.

34. *Jordan Times*, March 12, 1997.

35. Ibid.

36. Jordan TV (FBIS online), February 26; *Jordan Times*, March 1, 12, 1997. Quotes are from English text of Hussein's letter as published in the *Jordan Times*, March 12, 1997.

37. *Al-Aswaq*, April 22; *al-Sharq al-Awsat*, April 26, 1998.

38. Jordan TV (FBIS online), May 20, 1998.

39. Fahd al-Fanik in *al-Ra'y*, September 28, 1998.

40. Jordan TV (FBIS online), October 18, 1998.

41. Musa al-Kaylani in *Jordan Times*, October 12, 1996.

42. Susser, "Jordan," *MECS*, vol. XX (1996), p. 446; Tariq al-Tall, "Al-ustura wa-su al-fahm fi al-alaqat al-Urdunniyya-al-Filastiniyya" (The myth and misunderstanding of Jordanian-Palestinian relations), *al-Siyasa al-Filastiniyya*, no. 12 (Winter 1996), p. 160; Kumar Malhotra, "Jordan Learns to Live with Iraq," *Middle East International*, December 20, 1996, pp. 19–20; David Butter, "Economic Recovery Puts Down Roots," *Middle East Economic Digest*, January 3, 1997, p. 5.

43. Jordan TV, February 24, 1998.

44. *Jordan Times*, January 4, 19, 20, February 18, September 27, October 1, December 30; *al-Ra'y*, January 21; *al-Sharq al-Awsat*, February 19, November 10, 1997.

45. *Al-Dustur*, May 18; *al-Ra'y*, May 27, June 29; *Jordan Times*, May 28, June 8; Jordan TV (FBIS online), June 7, 1997.

46. *Al-Hayat*, March 29; *Jordan Times*, March 31, 1997.

47. Radio Monte Carlo (FBIS online), January 24, 25; *al-Quds al-'Arabi*, January 28; *al-Urdunn*, March 8, July 5; *Shihan*, May 3–9; *al-Majd*, May 19; *Jordan Times*, September 11–12, 1997.

48. *Al-Hayat*, May 3, 1997.

49. *Al-Quds al-'Arabi*, February 18; *al-Dustur*, March 24, 31; *al-Majd*, March 31; *Jordan Times*, April 13, June 28, 1997.

50. Radio Amman (FBIS online), November 1; *al-Dustur*, November 2; *Jordan Times*, November 2, 12, 13–14; *al-Aswaq*, November 11, 1997.

51. *Jordan Times*, November 22, 23, 24, 1997.

52. *Jordan Times*, December 13; Radio Amman (FBIS online), December 17; *al-Sharq al-Awsat*, December 19, 1997.

53. *Jordan Times*, December 10, 13, 16, 20; *al-Dustur*, December 14, 15, 20; Jordan TV (FBIS online), December 21, 1997.

54. Jordan TV, January 19; Iraqi News Agency (FBIS online), January 19, 21; *Shihan*, January 24–30, 1998.

55. Minister of Interior Nadhir Rashid in an interview with *al-Majalla*, March 22–28, 1998; *Jordan Times,* January 23, 1999.

56. Jordan TV, February 8; Middle East Broadcasting Corporation (MBC TV), London (FBIS online), February 9, 1998.

57. *Al-Aswaq,* January 19; Israel TV Channel 2 (FBIS online), January 30; *al-Sharq al-Awsat,* February 3, 1998.

58. Radio Amman (FBIS online), January 31, 1998.

59. Jordan TV (FBIS online), February 21, 1998.

60. MBC TV (FBIS online), February 1; *al-Ra'y,* February 10, 1998.

61. Jordan TV (FBIS online), February 10; *al-Majd,* February 16; *al-Dustur,* February 17; Radio Monte Carlo (FBIS online), February 20, 1998.

62. MBC TV (FBIS online), March 26, 1998.

63. MBC TV (FBIS online), February 22, 1998.

64. Jordan TV, February 24; Radio Amman, February 27; Radio Amman (FBIS online), June 6, 1998.

65. Jordan TV, February 24; Radio Monte Carlo (FBIS online), March 2, 1998.

66. *Al-Ra'y,* May 12, 1998.

67. *Al-Ittihad* (FBIS online), May 29; *al-Quds al-'Arabi,* June 1; *al-Sabil,* June 9–15; *al-Sharq al-Awsat,* July 27, 30, 1998.

68. JNA, November 11; Jordan TV, November 12; *al-Ahram,* December 3; Agence France Presse (FBIS online), December 20; *al-Dustur,* December 21, 1998.

69. Foreign Minister 'Abd al-Ilah al-Khatib to *al-Hadath,* December 28, 1998.

70. Radio Baghdad (FBIS online), December 26; *al-Dustur,* December 27, 1998.

71. Jordan TV (FBIS online), December 27, 1998.

72. MBC TV, December 27; *al-Bayyan* (FBIS online), December 29, 1998.

73. *Jordan Times,* February 11, 1999.

74. *Al-Hayat,* February 12; *Jordan Times,* February 25, March 15, 1999.

75. *Jordan Times,* February 28, 1999.

76. *Al-Sharq al-Awsat,* January 18, 1998.

77. *Al-Ra'y, al-Quds al-'Arabi,* June 5; *al-Watan al-'Arabi,* June 12; *al-Dustur,* July 1, 1998.

78. *Shihan,* October 10–16; JNA (FBIS online), October 18, 1998.

79. Jordan TV (FBIS online), October 13; *al-Bilad,* October 14; Radio Amman (FBIS online), October 18, 19, 1998.

80. Radio Amman (FBIS online), October 5, 1998.

81. Hassan in an interview with *Milliyet* (FBIS online), October 14, 1998.

82. *Shihan*, October 31–November 6, 1998.

83. *Shihan*, November 7–13, 1998.

84. *Jordan Times*, February 15, 1999.

85. Musa al-Kaylani in *Jordan Times*, April 24, 1999.

86. *Ha'aretz*, July 27, 30, August 1, 1999.

Summary and Conclusion

During the last fifty years, the frequently underestimated resilience of the Hashemites, together with the strategic backing and subvention of those supporting the status quo in Jordan, have outweighed the political hostility, military threats, economic sanctions, and subversion of the kingdom's opponents. This was, at times, aided by a certain lack of resolve on the part of at least some of the kingdom's enemies who were never entirely sure whether they consistently sought the overthrow of the regime and the consequent assumption of responsibility for Jordan's long front with Israel, or whether their interest was merely in pressuring King Hussein to change course. All these factors explain not only the prolonged stability of the state, but also the regime's enhanced image of a survivor. This image, in turn, augmented the leadership's deterrence capability against its domestic opponents, who were at times restrained by the possibility—real or imagined—of foreign intervention when the regime seemed seriously endangered. This was the case with the Palestinian opposition in the early 1960s, as with the Muslim fundamentalist opposition at present.[1]

Jordan's geopolitical centrality has proven both a liability and an asset to the regime. References by Jordanian leadership to the kingdom being located in a "killing zone," or to its "geopolitically thankless position," reflect Jordan's encirclement by neighbors that are relatively more powerful and capable of inflicting a wide array of extremely damaging penalties on the vulnerable kingdom—from political subversion, economic sanctions, or blockades, to "demographic aggression" or outright military invasion and conquest. Jordan therefore depends on the development of strong political and economic ties with an external power, and always with at least some of its neighbors, to ensure its survival.

As Prince Hassan often maintained, "being a small nation in the heart of a volatile region inclines one toward moderation and the middle ground . . . chart[ing] a consistently moderate and centrist course."[2] This has meant avoiding the potential hazards of the kingdom's location by eschewing provocation, forging political alliances and bilateral economic ties, and promoting transit trade, all of which serve to preserve the kingdom as a secure *terra media* in strategic, political, economic, and philosophical terms.

Yet this very same geopolitical centrality, as an asset rather than a liability, has afforded Jordan the essential room to maneuver to secure its interests. For instance, its long border with Israel has lent the kingdom crucial importance to its Arab neighbors during both peace and war: in wartime, Jordanian territory or airspace was used by other Arab states against Israel, and conversely Israel used Jordanian airspace against other Arab states; during times of peace, Jordan's Arab neighbors tend to see the kingdom as a potential bridge to Israeli penetration of the Arab world or as an Arab asset in promoting Israeli isolation. In both cases, Jordan may potentially benefit rather than suffer from the attentions of its neighbors. Jordanian leaders, analysts, and commentators refer time and again to the advantages inherent in the kingdom's pivotal location, lending it an importance—in terms of regional security or trade—that is greater than its size, intrinsic power, or wealth would normally warrant. To quote Hassan again:

> Historically, Jordan attained most of its importance because it was part of a wider area; it was the hinge, so to speak, that linked the sharply contrasted zones that lay to north and south, east and west. The political developments that began with the advent of the twentieth century once again placed Jordan at the center of events, and brought into high relief its potential regional role as a 'middle ground,' in more senses than one, in the Arab East.[3]

Jordan's intimate and multidimensional relationship with the Palestinians has always been, and still remains, one of the most crucial of what Hassan termed, these "hinges." Jordan was born out of the Palestinian question and has been tied by an umbilical cord to its fortunes and misfortunes from the inception of the Jewish–Arab struggle for Palestine. From time immemorial, the geographical factor has been conducive to the development of strong administrative, social, and commercial relationships between peoples on both banks of the Jordan River. Indeed, historically, relations on the East–West axis—between northern, central, and southern Jordan and the corresponding areas in Palestine—were far closer than those that linked these areas to one another on the North–South axis.[4]

Jordan's interests in Palestine, stemming from the kingdom's proximity coupled with the expansionist ambition of King 'Abdallah I, led Jordan to occupy and subsequently annex the West Bank in the first Arab–Israeli war of 1948. Although 'Abdallah achieved his political ambition with this action, the war resulted in a demographic and political transformation of his kingdom. In fact, Jordan has suffered more than other states from the demographic fallout of the Arab–Israeli conflict as hundreds of thousands of Palestinians took refuge in the kingdom (on both banks) in 1948 and again in 1967. There are today far more Palestinians in Jordan than in the West Bank, and possibly almost as many as in the West Bank and Gaza combined. It is, therefore, virtually impossible to conceive of a lasting and stable solution to the Palestinian question that does not forge some association between the East and West Banks. The West Bank is land-locked between Israel and Jordan; the more Israel disengages, and the more the Palestinians wish to reduce their dependence on Israel, so the West Bank will become increasingly dependent on Jordan. There are simply no other alternatives if Israel and the Palestinians do indeed choose to pursue the course of so-called "separation."

If, until 1967, Washington's interest in the Hashemite

Kingdom was born of the fear that an unstable Jordan might invite Israel's takeover of the West Bank producing seismic repercussions, the major U.S. interest in post-1967 Jordan shifted to advancing the Arab–Israeli peace process. From the outset, Jordan, because of its geopolitical position, demographic composition, historical involvement in the Palestinian issue, and relative moderation toward Israel was seen by the United States "as an essential part of the solution" to the Arab–Israeli conflict. As one historian has noted, "The attention and solicitations directed toward Jordan by the United States because of the Arab–Israeli conflict . . . have given Jordan a stature nearly equal to that of much larger, more powerful states, like Egypt, or vastly more wealthy ones, like Saudi Arabia."[5]

This stature did not necessarily provide for a harmonious U.S.–Jordanian meeting of the minds on the issues at hand, but neither did the differences between the two sides undermine Jordan's centrality to American peacemaking in the region. The kingdom was, instead, taken for granted. Offered the opportunity to participate in the Palestinian dimension of the Camp David accords without any prior consultation, for example, the Jordanians were insulted and they declined, especially as they were unable to secure an American guarantee for an Israeli withdrawal from the West Bank. But having rejected this offer, Jordan found itself in the rather desirable position of being courted and pressured by both supporters and opponents of Camp David. The kingdom eventually came down on the side of the opponents of the agreement, who were well endowed with Arab subventions to help maintain this position.[6]

The Reagan Plan of September 1982, in the wake of Israel's invasion of Lebanon, did offer Jordan a much-improved version of Camp David in the form of a Jordanian–Palestinian federation. The plan expressed the "firm view" of the United States that self-government by the Palestinians of the West Bank and Gaza, "in association with Jordan, offers the best chance for a durable, just, and lasting peace." It also specified the opposition of the United States to the establishment of an independent Palestinian state and to the continued occupation of the West Bank and Gaza by Israel.[7] But Jordan failed to achieve coordination with the Palestine Liberation Organization (PLO) in this regard, and Israel, having invaded Lebanon to crush the PLO and thereby secure its own hold over the West Bank, had no intention of offering the West Bank to either the Jordanians or to the PLO.

Jordan was similarly indispensable to American preparations for the Madrid conference in late 1991 in providing the essential "umbrella" for Palestinian participation. And although the Jordanians initially feared that the 1993 Oslo agreement signified a major historic shift in Israel's attitude toward the kingdom, these fears were apparently calmed by Yitzhak Rabin, who developed an exceptionally intimate strategic rapport with King Hussein.

Jordan's geopolitical centrality has indeed accorded the kingdom strategic importance that has remained intact in the face of frequently changing circumstances. Trans-Jordan initially had "little meaning beyond its importance to British strategy and imperial communications," and its significance naturally declined "when British interests changed or when British power itself receded."[8] But the Arab–Israeli conflict and the struggle for Palestine reaffirmed the kingdom's pivotal role for additional reasons. For instance, Jordan's utility to Israel as a *cordon sanitaire* was almost equaled by the importance that Israel's adversaries in the Arab world attached to the kingdom as a platform for the invasion of Israel, or alternatively, as an indirect approach for an Israeli invasion of Syria. Although Jordan's military is not the most powerful in the region by a wide margin, it is certainly the most highly respected and professional military force in the Arab world. The strategic importance of Jordanian territory, together with its military power, have therefore been almost as crucial to Syria as they have been to Israel, albeit for diametrically opposite reasons.

For much of its duration, the Arab–Israeli conflict coex-
isted with the Cold War which, quite aside from the former,
"also attracted the attention of the United States . . . in rough
proportion to real or imagined Soviet inroads in the area.
This, too, had the effect of giving an importance to Jordan
that was out of proportion to the intrinsic size and power of
the kingdom."[9] The inter-Arab struggle between the pro-
Western monarchies and the pro-Soviet revolutionaries that
Malcolm Kerr so aptly termed the "Arab Cold War" added
another dimension to the competition between the superpowers. Consequently, throughout much of the 1950s and
1960s, Jordan enjoyed a generally enhanced stature in the
eyes of the Western powers and their regional allies, especially Saudi Arabia.

The June 1967 War, however, was a watershed in the an-
nals of the modern Middle East. Egypt's humiliating defeat
was an irreversible setback for Gamal Abdul Nasser and his
messianic brand of pan-Arabism. The dichotomy of old, between "progressives" and "reactionaries," became irrelevant
overnight as Arab regimes of both persuasions were stranded
together in the same boat of ignominious defeat, equally dependent on the handouts of the wealthy Gulf states. Ideology
lost much of its potency in inter-Arab affairs; pan-Arabism
receded in favor of the legitimized notion of an Arab territorial state and the sober, naked pursuit of *raison d'état*. Noted
one observer, "unquestionably, such a style of politics is far
more congruent with the national interests of Jordan and its
own *modus operandi* than the volatile and vehemently ideological style of previous periods in inter-Arab relations."[10] But
this transformation in Arab politics also had its downside.
Jordan and Saudi Arabia breathed a sigh of relief after having been released from the revolutionary challenge of Nasser,
but the corollary of this release was the eventual decline of
Jordan's importance to Saudi Arabia in a relatively more re-
laxed state of inter-Arab affairs.

The end of the Cold War and the gradual replacement of
the Arab–Israeli conflict with Arab–Israeli diplomacy could po-

tentially have diminished some of Jordan's former regional significance to the United States as well.[11] Oslo clearly altered Jordan's role as indispensable partner for Israel in the pursuit of a settlement with the Palestinians. But the kingdom nevertheless remains a key, in the eyes of both Israel and the United States, to a moderate, stable, overall Palestinian solution.

The 1990s were, however, a period of strategic discomfort for Jordan. The United States remained Jordan's protector of last resort, but alliances in the Fertile Crescent were far more difficult to form. The kingdom's Arab neighbors had lost much of their political, strategic, and economic attractiveness. Syria was not a reliable ally, Iraq was incapacitated by the sanctions regime, and the Saudis were less willing to be of assistance with financial handouts. This reality made the option of peace with Israel almost unavoidable. As the Jordanians would have it, peace between Israel and Jordan, and between Israel and the Palestinians, poses neither a military nor a demographic threat, sparing Jordan the need to seek strategic depth in (and dependence on) Iraq or Syria. Peace buttressed by a strategic understanding between Israel and Jordan, on the contours of a Palestinian solution that would pose a threat to neither Jerusalem nor Amman, would provide Jordan with an even more profound sense of security. This kind of understanding seemed to exist between King Hussein and Rabin, but it eluded Hussein and Binyamin Netanyahu. So far, more than five years after the signing of the peace treaty, the economic dividends of peace have also fallen way below Jordanian expectations. If Israel was supposed to provide essential strategic and economic compensation for the shortcomings of Jordan's Arab brethren, it has yet to do so.

This has been doubly distressing for the Jordanians whose strategic discomfort has been coupled with socioeconomic trials and tribulations. The kingdom's economy is struggling to make ends meet, fighting a chronic imbalance between resources and population whereby economic growth can barely keep pace with population growth, if at all. Whatever Jordan cannot obtain from its association with Israel, it is bound to seek from the United States, and/or from a shift toward the Arab hinterland (especially Syria and Iraq).

In the meantime, since American and Arab aid is more difficult to obtain, Jordan has been forced into a strict International Monetary Fund (IMF) economic restructuring program. Tight-fisted budgeting and reductions in private consumption have caused widespread hardship as Jordan is gradually weaned from its addiction to foreign aid. Because the regime is now less capable of fulfilling its distributional role of remunerating longstanding loyalist constituencies, economic hardship and disaffection among some of the regime's traditional bedrocks of support have been the result. Although IMF recommendations are probably better for the country in the long run, Jordan has always preferred budgetary support over biting the bullet of structural economic reform with its attendant and immediate social and political stress.

In the interim, to smooth over the difficult economic readjustment, Jordan is still desperately trying to obtain infusions of aid—in addition to relief from its extremely burdensome foreign debt—from the United States and the West. As to aid requested, the Jordanians provide a variety of justifications, not least of which is its contribution to regional stability.

The almost universal recognition of Jordan's geopolitical centrality and concomitant stabilizing effect on the mosaic of Middle Eastern states has evolved over time. Whether it will continue to exist in the long run is a moot question. Nevertheless, one might risk an assessment. Considering the historical record, the inherent vagaries and volatility of regional politics and the dependence of external states on the area's resources, it is quite likely that Jordanian stability will continue to be of paramount interest to major powers both inside and outside the region. For most states, the Hashemite regime is preferable to any of the alternatives—fundamentalist or otherwise. Moreover, a collapse of the regime and the violent scramble for the spoils that would likely ensue between Syria and Iraq, or between either one—or both together—against Israel, could have potentially horrendous consequences for the entire region. Few, if any, have an interest in such a catastrophic turn of events. Jordan is no longer needed as a barrier against Arab revolutionaries or Soviet expansionism. But the kingdom's role as regional stabilizer among the Fertile Crescent states and between Arabs and Israelis remains as crucial as ever.

The impressive turnout of foreign dignitaries for King Hussein's funeral in February 1999, one of the largest gatherings of world leaders ever seen, was more than a gesture of respect to a great leader. It was an unprecedented demonstration of support by the international community for Jordan's well-being in the form of "a dazzling roster of presidents, prime ministers, princes and sheiks."[12] The United States was represented not only by President Clinton but by former Presidents Carter, Ford, and Bush in what U.S. National Security Adviser Samuel Berger described as "an extremely strong statement to the people of Jordan that America stands with them during this difficult period."[13]

After the funeral, commitments of aid to the kingdom came from every direction, and there were consequently no undue serious shocks to Amman's currency market. Aside from the U.S. pledge to increase its level of aid to Jordan, similar commitments were made by Britain and Japan. The United Arab Emirates deposited $150 million in the Jordanian Central Bank to shore up the dinar, and the IMF promised to speed up a new aid package to boost Jordan's struggling economy: The three-year plan, tied to further fiscal restraint and economic reform, is to provide Jordan with more than $150 million a year and pave the way for the Paris Club of Western European creditor nations to agree to an additional rescheduling of the kingdom's debt.[14]

But a concerted effort by King 'Abdallah II to quickly translate the expression of international goodwill into comprehensive debt forgiveness was less productive than the Jordanians had initially hoped. The wealthier states of the West seemed to have adopted a position that combined those of the IMF and the Saudis: they would serve as Jordan's ultimate insurance against economic collapse, but would not simply meet the Jordanians' financial obligations with generous donations or debt write-offs. Nor would the West provide aid that was not linked to serious efforts by the Jordanians themselves to introduce substantive economic reforms (liberalization, privatization, tax reform, and the like). Such reform was deemed essential if Jordan was to increase its capacity to repay at least some of its debt and to eventually reduce the kingdom's dependence on foreign aid. 'Abdullah's efforts to "persuade world leaders who had showered sympathy on Jordan to cough up cash as well as condolences"[15] were, therefore, only partially successful. Potential donors were presumably well aware of what Jordanian economic analysts no longer tried to disguise: the skillful manipulation of external interest in the kingdom's stability in order to obtain aid, which was often squandered.[16]

Even so, the international community has by no means been indifferent toward Jordan's economic distress. According to a 1998 World Bank report, Jordan had benefited from more donor support per capita than any other country of equal size and income level.[17] In May 1999, the Paris Club agreed to restructure more than $800 million of Jordan's foreign debt, while more than $300 million more was rescheduled by countries outside the club.[18] This was followed in June by the G-7 (major industrialized nations) agreement to include Jordan—although classified as a middle-income country—on the list of otherwise poorer states entitled to debt relief. The agreement was an exception justified by Jordan's "role as a moving force in the peace process and as a stabilizing factor for the whole Mideast region," and required the kingdom to enter into a series of bilateral negotiations with its creditors for the further rescheduling or cancellation of its debt. In July, in yet another gesture of international goodwill, the World Bank approved a further $210 million in loans to support development projects in Jordan.[19]

In light of the historical record, the smooth transition from Hussein to 'Abdallah II should come as no surprise. External interest in Jordan's continued stability, the cohesion of the country's ruling elite, and the loyalty of the security establishment and armed forces to the existing political order have been prime factors ensuring more than just "succession success."[20] They explain the overall historical longevity and stability of the Hashemite Kingdom of Jordan.

Notes

1. Asher Susser, "The Muslim Brotherhood in Jordan: Coexistence and Controlled Confrontation," in Meir Litvak, ed., *Islam and Democracy in the Arab World* (in Hebrew) (Tel Aviv: Hakibbutz Hameuchad Publishing House, 1998), p. 139.

2. Text of speech by Hassan in Prague on October 29, 1996, cited in *Jordan Times*, October 31–November 1, 1996.

3. Hassan Bin Talal, *Search for Peace: The Politics of the Middle Ground in the Arab East* (New York: St. Martin's Press, 1984), p. 75.

4. Center for Strategic Studies, *The Jordanian–Palestinian Relationship: The Domestic Dimension* (Amman: Center for Strategic Studies, University of Jordan, 1996), p. 5.

5. Adam Garfinkle, "Jordan in World Politics," in Joseph Nevo and Ilan Pappe, eds., *Jordan in the Middle East, 1948–1988: The Making of a Pivotal State* (London: Frank Cass, 1994), p. 285.

6. Gabriel Ben-Dor, "Jordan and Inter-Arab Relations: An Overview," in Nevo and Pappe, eds., *Jordan in the Middle East, 1948–1988*, p. 193.

7. Susser, "Jordan," *MECS*, vol. VI (1981–82), p. 682.

8. Mary Wilson, *King Abdullah, Britain and the Making of Jordan* (Cambridge: Cambridge University Press, 1987), pp. 213–214.

9. Garfinkle, "Jordan in World Politics," p. 285.

10. Ben-Dor, "Jordan and Inter-Arab Relations," p. 195.

11. Garfinkle, "Jordan in World Politics," pp. 300–302.

12. *Washington Post*, February 9, 1999.

13. *New York Times*, February 9, 1999.

14. *Jordan Times*, February 9, 20; *New York Times*, February 19, 1999.

15. *Economist*, July 10, 1999.

16. Riad al-Khouri in *Jordan Times*, February 18, 1999.

17. *New York Times*, February 19, 1999.

18. *Jordan Times*, May 22, 26, 1999.

19. *Jordan Times*, June 22, July 1, July 28; *Economist*, July 10, 1999.

20. Asher Susser, "The Succession Success," *New Republic*, February 22, 1999, p. 18.

Postscript

Popular at home and respected abroad,[1] 'Abdallah II in his first year on the throne has generally bolstered confidence in the monarchy and in its capacity to continue to serve as the institutional "unifying essence" of the state. With admirable determination, 'Abdallah has made great strides in reordering the kingdom's priorities, immediately recognizing the need to contend with Jordan's flagging economy above all else. Initial assessments that 'Abdallah was a "chip off the old block," possessing his father's "aura, charisma, charm [and] politesse,"[2] have been confirmed, both in terms of the intuitive cognition with which he has defined Jordan's problems and the resolve with which he has chosen to face them.

Father and son, although so similar in their intelligence, dynamism, and courage, are naturally separated by a generation gap. Hussein and 'Abdallah, common traits aside, have had to operate in totally different historical contexts, in which the reality and spirit of the times have changed dramatically. Hussein spent his formative years in power in the 1950s and early 1960s contending with the challenges of Nasserism and the Arab–Israeli conflict. For Hussein, it was crucial from his very first moment on the throne to devote himself to the regional and international battles of the day for the sake of self-preservation.

At the end of the century, however, after nearly fifty years at the helm and when regional and international changes had created both new domestic political imperatives and a pressing socioeconomic agenda, reordering Jordan's priorities did not come easily to the monarch. The post-Nasserist, post–Cold War, post–oil boom Middle East where the Arab–Israeli conflict was also winding down required a more inward-looking leadership. Whereas Hussein found it difficult in his last years to make that transition, 'Abdallah has done so with the same instinctive determination with which his father had faced down his own adversaries in the early years.

'Abdallah has shifted the emphasis from Jordan's regional involvement to the economic front, simultaneously embarking on the first cautious but calculated steps of elite expansion by involving members of the business community from the younger generation—Jordanians and Palestinians alike—in the reform process. These moves have not gone unopposed by some of the old guard. But 'Abdallah, more than twice Hussein's age when he ascended the throne, has established his authority with remarkable speed. He has also benefited from the guidance received from some of his father's former confidants and from the good fortune of being able to conduct himself within a regional and international order far more hospitable to Jordan than was the case in Hussein's early years.

International recognition of Jordan's stabilizing role now exists in a way that it did not in the 1950s. But 'Abdallah has not taken this for granted. On the contrary, he spent a considerable amount of time abroad in his first year as king cementing Jordan relations and his own personal ties with leaders in the United States, Europe, the Middle East, and the Far East. Rulers worldwide received him with the respect reserved for "important" states. Although 'Abdallah failed to extract the amounts of economic aid or the debt forgiveness for which he had initially hoped, he did manage to obtain very helpful debt rescheduling and to pave the way for Jordanian membership in the World Trade Organization.

'Abdallah has already established his image in Washington as an "emerging heavyweight"[3] among the new generation of Middle Eastern rulers (less so in the eyes of his father's Arab peers). With many of these younger men, from the Maghreb to the Gulf, he has developed a network of close ties. But 'Abdallah's real tests lie ahead. One challenge will be the extrication of Jordan from its economic crisis and the securing of sustainable economic growth that will outpace the natural increase of the Jordanian population. Another will be keeping the ever-sensitive relations between Jordanians and Palestinians in the kingdom on an even keel as Israel and the Palestinian Authority continue to negotiate the emergence of an independent Palestinian state on Jordan's doorstep.

This is a tall order. It will require the closing of the "digital gap" through a reorientation of Jordan's human capital toward the ultra-modern domains of information and high technology, while simultaneously engaging in domestic political finessing that may be extremely controversial. These challenges are fully recognized by the new monarch, but success is by no means guaranteed. Jordan's friends worldwide want to see 'Abdallah and Jordan succeed and will surely provide assistance in this regard. But at the end of the day, policies geared toward ameliorating domestic dissension, downsizing the bloated bureaucracy, revamping the economy, curbing corruption, and promoting family planning are matters with which only the Jordanians themselves can contend.

'Abdallah has the relative advantage of having to deal with the challenges of globalization and domestic political uneasiness, which are less immediately threatening to regime stability than was the threat of the fedayeen in the late 1960s, or of Syrian or United Arab Republic intelligence subversion in the heyday of Nasser. On the other hand, solutions to the present challenges are more complex and difficult to produce. It is easier to crush the opposition by force or to counter the mischief of foreign agents with one's own domestic intelligence organs than to develop the human capital, artificial intelligence, and information technology to secure a future in the global economy. This is all the more true when one must concurrently prevent—with the utmost care, tact, and mastery of the craft of politics—the exacerbation of Jordanian–Palestinian tensions on the East Bank.

'Abdallah II and his generation are perhaps better equipped than Hussein and the men of his time to make these essential transitions, but it remains for the younger men to prove that, in the long run, they can reign and rule like their fathers.

Notes

1. Jeffrey Goldberg, "Learning How to be King," *New York Times Magazine*, February 6, 2000.

2. *Washington Post*, February 6, 1999.

3. Goldberg, "Learning How to be King."